Developing a Vision for Ministry in the 21st Century

A church without vision is like a plane without wings . . . regardless of the energy and motion generated, it will never fly. Vision is a non-negotiable for a growing church!

In this important new book the author helps readers understand why vision is such a key foundation upon which church plans and activities must be built. He then leads us in the next important step: how to develop such a vision.

In my work as a church growth consultant I am constantly amazed at the timelessness of the Scripture: "Without a vision, the people perish." It's as true for today as it has been throughout history.

A vision provides the *energy* necessary for a church to move forward. When pastors and church leaders find it difficult to recruit volunteers, it is usually because the church lacks a clear vision. My experience is that churches with a vision have no shortage of people willing to help reach it. This is a book that will help leaders lead their people toward such a vision.

Developing a
Vision
for
Ministry
in the 21st Century

Aubrey Malphurs

Foreword
Haddon W. Robinson

Baker Books

A Division of Baker Book House Co
Grand Rapids, Michigan 49516

ISBN: 0-8010-6286-1

Seventh printing, January 1999

Printed in the United States of America

Library of Congress Cataloging-in-Publication Data
Malphurs, Aubrey.
    Developing a vision for ministry in the twenty-first century/
Aubrey Malphurs ; foreword by Haddon W. Robinson.
      p.   cm.
    ISBN 0-8010-6286-1
    1. Pastoral theology. 2. Christian leadership. I. Title.
BV4011.M36   1992
253—dc20   91-42503

For current information about all releases from Baker Book
House, visit our web site:
                  http://www.bakerbooks.com

To
My precious wife and family
Susan
Mike
Jen
David
Greg

Contents

Foreword, Haddon W. Robinson   9
Introduction   13

    1. It's a Must!   19
    2. What Are We Talking About?   29
    3. Giving Birth: Part 1   41
    4. Giving Birth: Part 2   55
    5. It's a Vision!   93
    6. Overcoming Initial Inertia   137
    7. Overcoming Obstinate Obstacles   157
    8. Wearing the Management Hat   187
    9. Bitter-Sweet   215

Worksheets
    Developing Your Vision   239
    Developing Vision Slogans   242
    Casting Your Vision   243
    Building a Team 1   245
    Building a Team 2   248
    Planning Your Ministry   250
    Preserving Your Vision   251

Endnotes   253

Foreword

In Robert Browning's poem "Paracelsus" a man travels toward a city, but it is surrounded by swirling mists. He thinks that he must have taken the wrong road and lost his way. But then the mist opens and for an instant he glimpses the spires of the city in the distance. Browning pens the triumphant lines:

> So long the city I desired to reach lay hid
> When suddenly its spires afar flashed through the circling
>   clouds,
> You may conceive my transport,
> Soon the vapours closed again, but I had seen the city!

A leader must have vision. We all see the shrouding mists, but leaders have seen the city. Leaders glimpse what others may not see and are captured by it. That's why they risk everything to reach the city.

Christian leaders do not have dreams in the night. Their visions belong to the day. Those who dream by night in the murky recesses of their minds wake and find their visions vanity; but the dreamers of the day are formidable men and women, for they receive their dreams from God with open eyes, and they believe that under God they can turn them into reality.

Since our vision must be God's vision, we must gain it from the Scriptures. Some devout women and men, however, have taken an unauthentic lead from their commitment to the Bible. They long for "the good old days" of the church when God was alive and well and when he rolled up his sleeves and worked miracles. Their vision amounts to going back to "the New Testament church."

But which New Testament congregations do they have in mind? These early churches were infested with heretics. Members were at each other's throats. Some were guilty of sexual sin and many rejected apostolic authority. If our vision lies in a return to a New Testament church, then there's good news. We've already arrived!

Let's face it. There were no "good old days" for the church. There were no favorable times and no better saints than there are today. While we may learn from the past, we cannot copy it. A vision for the church in the twenty-first century cannot come from going backward into the future.

Our vision must arise from recognizing what the transcendent, contemporary God wants to do for his church and through his church today. Having seen that, leaders can then envision what God will do in the place they serve—the congregation at Fifth and Main in a particular community. Strong leaders possess a vision as great as God and as specific as a zip code.

Leaders also communicate their vision to those who serve Christ with them. John Ruskin spoke of that service when he observed, "The greatest thing a human ever does in the world is to see something and tell others what he saw in a plain way. Hundreds can talk for one who can think, but thousands can think for one who can see. To see clearly and tell others clearly is poetry, prophecy, and religion all in one."

Leaders lift people's eyes to what matters. By bringing the eternal into time, they summon Christians to a different kind of service by giving them a different perspective. Leaders must not only see the city; they must also talk about it in plain words their followers can grasp and that grasp their followers.

Yet, seeing and communicating vision is not magic. Leaders can be better at leading than they are. Aubrey

Malphurs has written this helpful, down-to-ministry book that guides a thoughtful reader in developing a vision and inspiring others with it. One sure test of whether or not you are a leader is this: Does a book like this inflame you with indignation or fire your imagination? Leaders with enough imagination to capture reality will wear out this book as they develop a vision for ministry in the twenty-first century.

As Christian leaders we have something in common with Walt Disney. Soon after the completion of Disney World someone said, "Isn't it too bad that Walt Disney didn't live to see this!" Mike Vance, creative director of Disney Studios replied, "He did *see* it—that's why it's here."

Haddon W. Robinson
The Harold John Ockenga
Distinguished Professor of Preaching,
Gordon-Conwell Theological Seminary

Introduction

Pastor Bob was extremely discouraged with his ministry at the church. This was in bold contrast to when he first became its pastor.

He could not remember having been more excited about anything except when, in his freshman year at college, he had accepted Christ. A senior had befriended him, and they began to play tennis together. He had noticed Frank was different and that he carried a tattered Bible on the back seat of his old Chevrolet coupe. Eventually, their conversations turned from sports to spiritual things. For several months Frank answered Bob's questions, often in sessions that lasted until the early hours of the morning. Near the end of the term Bob embraced Jesus Christ as his Savior.

Life for Bob took on an entirely new dimension. He had gained a purpose for his life, which answered his questions and gave him direction for the future—his decision to pursue the ministry. After his conversion he had devoured his Bible and everything he could find that taught him the truths of the Scriptures. Then he formed a Bible study group in a friend's house off campus that grew significantly and which saw a number of students come to faith in Christ. Bob loved it. He knew God's hand was on his life, as he had never felt so significant and fulfilled. Also, it was in this group that he met someone very special. Her name was Mary.

After graduation from college, Bob married Mary and then attended seminary. Everything went smoothly the first year. Mary worked full time and Bob worked as the part-time youth director at a nearby small church. But then Mary announced that she was expecting their first child. Bob wanted Mary to stay at home with the baby, so he took a full-time job and arranged for a lighter load of classes at the seminary.

When Bob turned in the last paper in his last class, he breathed a sigh of relief. It had taken him four years to complete seminary rather than the usual three. His boss had worked his hours around his class schedule, but asked for some overtime in return. There was not a lot of time left for studies and his family. This placed a tremendous strain on him and his marriage. Several times he was not sure if he and Mary would make it financially or emotionally. Finally the worst part was behind them. He looked forward with great anticipation and excitement to being a pastor, which he had dreamed about in his last year in college and all through seminary. This dream had fueled the fire that kept him going.

He took a relatively new, growing church located in the suburbs of a sizable metropolitan city. The first year had been relatively problem free. He told Mary that in some ways it was comparable to their honeymoon. But in his second year all that began to change. As he thought about the various problems that had begun to surface, he was tempted to place the blame on others. But deep in his heart he realized that most of them stemmed from a lack of leadership on his part. It was not that he did not care about the people or did not want to lead the church; he wanted this desperately. The problem was that he simply did not know how. The seminary had taught him a lot about the Bible and theology, for which he was grateful. But few courses touched on leadership, and he had taken none in this area in college. He had to depend on what natural abilities God had given him and what he had learned from a position as an assistant manager at a fast-food restaurant during his year off between high school and college.

He knew deep down in his heart that in board meetings (which in private to Mary he referred to as "bored meetings") he was "winging it." And he suspected that certain men on the board knew it as well, although no one ever said anything that first year. He felt it in their looks when he had no answers for their questions regarding the direction of their church.

Bob respected these men. They were his age and had proved themselves excellent leaders in the marketplace. He often referred to them as "hard chargers." Though they had much in common with Pastor Bob, such as their age and commitment to Christ, these men grew dissatisfied with his leadership. They believed the ministry lacked direction, which they felt was critical to its future. They were all for Bob as a person and liked him and his preaching, but they wanted to know where the church was going. They asked some hard questions, such as, "What is our direction? Where will we be five or ten years from now? And what is your strategy to get us there?" Frankly, Pastor Bob did not have a clue.

The other men on the board did not seem to care about these matters. They were happy as long as Pastor Bob did not "rock the boat." But he sensed that the future of this church was with the hard chargers. At first he was frustrated, because he wanted to lead these men, but he did not know what to do. The more he worked with them, the more he realized his inabilities to lead them and to come up with solutions to the church's problems. At the same time, the church had begun to plateau. Others noticed and began to talk about it. His frustration gradually turned into discouragement. What would he do? Should he quit? Had he chosen the wrong profession?

Pastor Bob did not realize he was not alone. Numerous leaders like him, whether in the church or parachurch, struggle in their roles as leaders. This is clearly reflected in the fact that Christian institutions across the land have arrived at the end of the century exhausted and gasping for breath. Currently 80 to 85 percent of American churches are either plateaued or dying with no revival in sight. A considerable number of parachurch organizations are experiencing much the same.

A Gallup publication indicates that the number of unchurched Americans climbed to 44 percent as of 1988. Pollster George Barna sets the figure even higher. To make matters worse a number of cults and New Age religions are both filling the void and attracting the unchurched. In particular, the Mormons and Jehovah's Witnesses doubled their numbers between 1965 and 1985.

At the same time, there is hope in that a "new wind" is blowing across the horizon of American Christianity. It is the wind of vision. God is presently infusing a number of new leaders in various Christian organizations across the land with a profound, significant vision for the future. *Vision* is a word that has been borrowed from the marketplace, but it is also a good biblical concept. It is timely and critical to leaders because it has the potential to breathe fresh life into them and, thus, into their church or parachurch ministries. In short, there is hope, great hope, for leaders like Pastor Bob.

Vision in terms of ministry exists both on a personal and institutional level. Personal vision concerns itself directly with the individual leader's unique design, which helps immensely in determining his or her future ministry direction. It comes as the result of discovering his divine design from God. This unique design consists of spiritual gifts, natural talents, passion, temperament, leadership style, and so on. The discovery of personal vision helps Christians in general and leaders in particular to determine their future place of ministry within the body of Christ.

Institutional vision relates directly to the ministry of a particular Christian organization, whether a church or parachurch. Once leaders have determined their personal vision they identify with a ministry organization that has an institutional vision which aligns itself most closely with their personal vision. This has several advantages. One is that it lessens the likelihood of ministry burnout. Another is that through aligning with the similar vision of an institution the leader's personal vision accomplishes a greater impact, because it has the institution behind it.

Both personal and institutional visions are essential. This book is designed to help leaders like Pastor Bob develop a unique institutional vision for the organization they lead or are a part of. To accomplish this goal it is necessary to take six steps which make up the envisioning process. These steps correspond approximately to the nine chapters of the book.

The first step is to realize the importance of having a ministry vision. Here the question to be answered is, How vital is vision to ministry? Chapter 1 will present specific reasons why vision is essential to the success of any ministry that desires to be on the cutting edge in the twenty-first century.

The second step is to understand the definition of a ministry vision. Exactly what are we talking about? What does the term *vision* mean when used of a ministry? Chapter 2 will define vision and explain its key ingredients.

The third step is the process of developing, or "giving birth," to a vision. Chapter 3 focuses attention on the participants in the development stage. It will answer the question, Who in the ministry is responsible for "birthing" the vision? Chapter 4 takes leaders through the process of creating a vision statement tailor-made for their ministry. It also explains how leaders can know when they have such a vision and includes sample vision statements and slogans as catalysts for creativity.

The fourth step is communication of the vision. It is not enough to have a good vision. Leaders must cast and recast the vision in such a way that others are inspired to "own" and follow the vision. Chapter 5 will present various ideas to help leaders communicate their vision.

In the fifth step visionary leaders implement their visions. This focuses on the important area of leadership and the careful, patient construction of a leadership team to implement the vision. Chapter 6 helps the leader to recruit a committed, cooperative visionary team who will own the same vision and work together toward the realization of that vision. Chapter 7 also concerns the implementation of the vision through team building. However, this chapter focuses on empowering a committed, visionary team to overcome the obstinate obstacles they are sure to face on the way to the implementation of the vision.

While it is not an actual step in the envisioning process, I have included a section on the important area of management and the development of a ministry plan in particular. It is the plan that serves as a reality check on the dream and translates it into a working reality. But plans can be boring things that throw water on the flame of a good vision. Chapter 8 will help leaders develop visually attractive, marketable plans that motivate and recruit people for the ministry.

The last step is the preservation of a vision. Visionary people must know how to recognize and handle opposition and its fruit, discouragement. Failure in this area results in "early funerals," that is, the death of the vision and ultimately the ministry. The last chapter will help leaders recognize and deal with various "vision vampires," "vision vultures," and "vision firemen."

It's a Must!

The Importance of a Vision

What has gone wrong with Pastor Bob's ministry? Why has the ministry plateaued? What are the men on the board looking for when they want to know where the church will be five or ten years from now? Why is he preaching more but enjoying it less? In general the problem is that the church and these men are looking for a leader. They want someone whom they can respect to lead them into the twenty-first century. In particular the problem is vision. The missing vital element in Bob's leadership is vision. To lead these men, especially the hard chargers, he will need to articulate a profound vision for the church's future. But at this point in the ministry, Pastor Bob does not have a vision.

Vision is crucial to any ministry. Ministry without vision is like a surgeon without a scalpel, a cowboy who has lost his horse, a carpenter who has broken his hammer. To attempt a ministry without a clear, well-articulated vision is to invite a "stillbirth." Church and parachurch ministries may grow at the very beginning, but without a vision they are destined to plateau and eventually die. There are several reasons for this.

Direction

A vision provides a ministry with direction. It answers the question, Where is this ministry going? It brings the future into focus for both the leader and those who are a part of the ministry organization.

First, it is imperative that leaders like Pastor Bob know where they are going. I would define a Christian leader as a godly person (character) who knows where he or she is going (vision) and has followers (influence). Thus, vision is one of the three critical components of a leader's makeup.

Leaders must be able to articulate what God has called them to do. Not to be able to do so is to invite disaster. For example, some people will follow a so-called leader who does not know where he is going. The result is that they all wind up in the proverbial ditch. Also, a leader cannot develop a plan to implement the ministry without a clear target. As someone has said, "If you aim at nothing, you will hit it every time."

On numerous occasions leaders in the Bible demonstrated a leadership based on clear ministry direction. Moses demonstrated his acute knowledge of God's direction for the people of his generation when he appeared before Pharaoh and demanded their release (Exod. 5–7). Nehemiah demonstrated that he knew precisely where he was going when he presented his vision to King Artaxerxes (Neh. 2:5).

Second, the people who are a part of the organization must know where it is going. People cannot "focus on fog." If God's people are to accomplish great things for him, they must know what it is they are setting out to accomplish.

Most people who are a part of a ministry organization fall into one of three problematic categories of ministry direction. The largest category by far consists of ministries that have no vision and thus no idea where the ministry is headed. Most often they are maintenance ministries that are headed nowhere. Neither the leaders nor the members have any direction. If the organization is a parachurch ministry and dependent on outside funding, it will soon die. However, if it is a church, it may continue another ten to twenty years in this condition until the majority of the members die off and there is no one to replace them.

Another problematic category consists of ministries with multiple visions. These are organizations led by a leadership team in which each member has his or her own unique vision for the ministry. One may envision an evangelism orientation for the ministry. Another may envision a discipleship orientation. While there is nothing wrong with any of these visions, an organization can only sustain a single ministry vision. Most often a ministry with multiple visions ends with a split. Actually, the split was already cooking on the "back burner" from the very beginning of the organization; it only needed sufficient time to boil over and cause a major ministry disaster.

A final problematic category is ministries with a single, clear vision. The problem is that the vision is the wrong vision. An example would be a parachurch ministry whose vision is the Great Commission. While many parachurch ministries have sprung into existence because of some major inadequacy in the church, this does not mean that God intends to replace the church with parachurch. By definition the parachurch is to minister alongside of the church, not in place of the church.

Another example would be a church whose vision is not the Great Commission but some element of the Commission. For example, one church is known in a community for its in-depth Bible teaching, another for its outstanding pulpiteer. A third church has a reputation for a strong family ministry, while a fourth has an outstanding counseling program. This attracts people to what I call "bunny hop" or "consumer" Christianity. The result most often is transfer growth, that is, the repopulation of the larger churches at the expense of the depopulation of the smaller churches in the area. Another result is that people "shop around" at the various churches according to present felt needs without any commitment to a particular body. In fact, George Barna predicts:

> In the coming decade, however, increasing numbers of people will instead select between two and five local

churches and consider these to be their group of home churches. On any given weekend, they will determine which church to attend according to their own most keenly-felt needs, and the programs each of their favored churches has to offer.[1]

By way of contrast, early in his ministry Nehemiah made a point of communicating the vision to the people under his leadership, the remnant in Jerusalem, so that they would know precisely where they were going (Neh. 2:17, 18). Joshua did the same shortly after he replaced Moses as the new leader of Israel (Josh. 1:10, 11).

Unity

Scripture places great emphasis on the importance of unity among God's people. Indeed, God has sprinkled passages on unity throughout the Bible. An institutional vision is one of the critical components of unity in ministry. The vision affects at least two areas of organizational unity.

The first area of unity is the recruitment of ministry personnel. A vision signals to all who desire to be a part of the ministry precisely where that ministry is going. This gives potential participants an opportunity to both examine and determine their own personal visions in light of their gifts, passions, temperaments, talents, and abilities. They can decide in advance if their personal visions closely match the organization's direction, or whether they should look elsewhere for ministry opportunities. In either case, this recruitment protects continued ministry cohesion because it heads off potential problems before they are conceived and born into the ministry.

The second area of unity is the retention of ministry personnel. This itself naturally has two potential results. One is harmony on the ministry team. New Testament ministry is team ministry. A good ministry team consists of richly gifted people with diverse personalities who make significant but different contributions to the ministry. That is why a wise leader will recruit staff members who have strong gifts in areas where he is less gifted. The problem is that this diversity supplies the fuel for potential conflict among those on the ministry team. Each temperament has a different perspective on life and, therefore, a different opinion about how things should be accomplished.

The solution to this problem is a clear, single ministry vision. Vision functions as a cohesive factor; it holds the team together. Although the team consists of people who are creatively different, a major reason they joined the team initially is because they passionately held to the same vision. If nurtured carefully, the result is that each person appreciates and values the other because he or she sees how each, though different, is necessary and contributes in a unique way to the accomplishment of their vision. They realize that they all need each other if anything significant is going to take place. This, in effect, mirrors such passages on the importance of diversity within unity as 1 Corinthians 12:20–22 and Ephesians 4:15, 16.

Vision is vital to another area of the retention of ministry personnel. If regularly communicated, the vision serves as a constant reminder to those in the ministry of the direction they have agreed to pursue together as a team. This is important, because life is full of changes. People and ministries often change and adjust their direction. Clarity of the vision gives the people who make up the organization a chance to re-evaluate the organization's direction in light of their own gifts and personal directions in life. If the forecast is eventual disharmony, a person can seek another opportunity more in line with his or her own vision. But whether a person contemplates joining the organization or is already involved in that organization, a clear knowledge of ministry direction best enhances organizational harmony.

Change

Few would deny that we live in times of tremendous change, and researchers tell us, "You ain't seen nothin' yet!" For example, Barna writes that Americans have only 3 percent of the general information that will be available to us by the year 2010.[2] Yet some ministry organizations continue to plod along oblivious to the massive changes taking place all around them. Others are aware of the changes but are baffled as to how they should respond. And some seriously question if they should respond at all.

Many voices warn that the fact of change is no longer the issue. The real issue is how the church and the parachurch in the 90s and the next century will handle this torrent of change. Those who handle it poorly will, most likely, not survive the 90s, but those who handle it well will make significant advances for the Savior that will surpass those of the 90s and realize new opportunities in the twenty-first century.

The key to relevant, constructive change for the future church is the development of a well-articulated ministry vision. Ministry organizations that have developed a clear, focused vision for their future, who know where they are going, are able to cope effectively with change in at least two ways.

First, they are able to respond to and take advantage of this avalanche of change coming from outside the organization. Because vision supplies focus and clarity, they are able to chart a clear course through the fog of change. They know which changes are beneficial and which pose potential disaster for the organization. Consequently, they will be able to make wise choices about what to accept and reject in terms of the ministry's future.

In addition, they will be able to direct the tidal wave of change to their advantage. If they know where they are going, change can provide them with a number of new, attractive options to get them there. Change does not have to be bad nor destructive. Along with change come new and exciting opportunities. These can be put to work to catalyze and motivate a ministry to new accomplishments for the Savior. For example, a raging, rain-swollen river has the capability to kill and destroy. However, that same potential, if brought under control, can be directed to turn turbines which generate power and all kinds of new, productive opportunities in life.

Second, this environment of tremendous change presents a ministry organization with an opportunity to launch needed changes from within. Change in the world outside an organization necessitates change inside the organization if it is to stay relevant and continue to have an impact in its area of ministry. While change for change's sake has some merit, initiating change without direction could be just as damaging to an organization as no change at all. Consequently, a ministry organization with a clear, focused vision is in a position to initiate wise change that will help to accomplish the ministry's purpose.

Motivation

Not much happens without a vision. Not much was happening in Jerusalem in Nehemiah's day. The walls were broken down and the gates lay charred by fire, and no one was motivated to do anything about it (Neh. 1:3). Then Nehemiah arrived with a vision from God. It is important to observe the overwhelming response of the remnant of Israel who were motivated by Nehemiah's first casting of that vision: "Then they said, 'Let us arise and build.' So they put their hands to the good work" (Neh. 2:18).

A good vision motivates. It is the lifeblood and the driving force behind a ministry. It is the fuel that lights a fire under the people; it enables leaders to stop putting out fires and start igniting fires. The vision from God has the potential in a ministry to turn a maintenance mentality into a ministry mentality. It catalyzes custodians and caretakers into ministers and leaders.

An important question in leadership circles today is, How do you motivate people for ministry? How do you move them in the direction you want them to go? Some leaders motivate directly by attempting to follow certain cardinal principles of motivation. However, others do not attempt to motivate people directly. Instead, they concentrate on motivating themselves, because the motivation of persons in highly visible positions of leadership is contagious. Hence, they model motivation.

But what motivates the leaders? Their motivation comes from God in the form of clear, compelling, and exciting visions of what God would have them to do. They are intensely vision driven.[3] It would seem obvious that this is what happened to Nehemiah. First, God gave him the vision. This so affected his life that, in turn, when he communicated his vision to others such as Artaxerxes and the Jerusalem remnant, God used his intensity to rally them in his behalf.

Thus vision serves a rather unique function. It not only provides an organization with its direction; at the same time it supplies the energy to move the organization in that direction.

Giving

An often ignored truth in ministry circles is that a vision is the key to the members' giving of money. Many organizations attempt to raise funds by appealing to their constituency on the basis of need and not vision. The problem is that most people are not motivated to give to meet needs. If need motivated giving, then most people would be givers, and most ministries would not have any financial shortages.

Wise donors view giving as a serious investment of God's money. Therefore, many donors view giving to ministries that constantly appeal primarily on the basis of need much the same as investing in an organization that is in the red. People do not want to give regularly to bail out a ministry that faces or has been inundated with debt. But people are moved to give to organizations that project a clear, well-articulated vision.

The reason is that the vision says the ministry is not static but dynamic. It is going somewhere. It is not hopelessly trapped in the cobwebs of yesterday's debts but is focused on the exciting possibilities of the future. Vision communicates that while God is doing something exciting now, the best is yet to come.

Not only does vision motivate people to give of their finances or treasure, it encourages them to give of their time and talent. Both are critical to the life of any ministry organization. Most ministry organizations such as the church depend heavily on volunteers. Yet today's generation is so short on extra time for ministry that they are not able to use their talents for ministry effectively. They value and cherish their time and, therefore, many will give of their treasure before their time and talents when actually all three are needed.

After Nehemiah communicated his vision, the people of God responded not only with their treasure (Neh. 7:70–72) but with their time and talents (detailed in Neh. 3). This happened most likely because vision ultimately affects people's values and felt needs. People find time in their busy schedules for that which they value. Nehemiah's people valued the concept of rebuilding the city gates because they symbolized the spiritual decline of Israel at that time. People also respond to visions that address their felt needs. Nehemiah's vision found his people in dire need of deliverance from their distress and reproach (Neh. 1:3).

Evaluation

An essential part of any growing, dynamic ministry is evaluation. Whatever an organization does must constantly be evaluated through the lens of its vision. Evaluation poses the purpose question, Why are we doing what we are doing? Vision supplies the answer.

A glaring weakness in far too many ministry organizations is the lack of persistent evaluation of what they do. Chief of offenders has been the church. Perhaps this is the result of the church's natural resistance to being evaluated in a similar manner to secular organizations such as those in the marketplace that place a high premium on quality control. It is no longer acceptable to respond to the *why* question with the timeworn answer, Because we've always done it this way. In a sophisticated world that demands quality as well as quantity, this means that everything the church does should be traced back to and explained in light of its vision. The answer to the *why* question is, We believe this will best facilitate the accomplishment of the vision of this church.

Consequently, the church is structured and organized around its vision. The sermons that are preached and the lessons taught all contribute in a demonstrative way to the accomplishment of the vision. For example, a church that has as a major part of its vision the reaching of nonchurched lost people will organize a number of its events and ministries for them. It will schedule certain meetings at times that are attractive to nonchurched people. The sermons and teaching will be relevant to the nonchurched and presented in language they can understand.

Of course, the major test of an organization's commitment to its stated vision is the budget. An evaluation of the budget will quickly show any discrepancies. For example, if the organization is committed to reaching unchurched people, this will be reflected proportionately in the budget. While almost everyone is inclined to vote for such areas as evangelism, the proof of the pudding is in the budget.

A well-developed institutional vision is a must for any ministry that desires to be on the cutting edge in the twenty-first century. Once leaders realize how crucial is vision, the next step is to define the term.

2

What Are We Talking About?

Definition of Vision

Pastor Bob is a very insightful, intelligent young man. In spite of all the hours he worked to support his family during his seminary days, he still managed to graduate with honors. Therefore, he knew he needed to do something about his faltering ministry and was willing to begin. He asked one of his sharpest leaders, Jack, to join him for lunch.

After a few pleasantries, Bob nervously got to the point with a series of rapid-fire questions: "What is it you guys are looking for? In your opinion, why are things not going well in the church? What am I doing wrong? Do you have any suggestions?"

Jack's response was equally to the point. As if he had been waiting for these questions, he looked Bob in the eyes and said, "I don't think you know where you are going with the church, and, quite frankly, I find it very frustrating to try to follow a man who does not know where he is going. In short, you lack vision."

This was hard on Pastor Bob's ego. After all, he was supposed to be a leader. That was what the church had hired him for. However, Bob realized that he did not know what Jack was talking about when he said that he lacked vision. Certainly, he was not referring to some kind of extra, special revelation from God; Jack was theologically sophisticated enough to know better than that. Jack read the bewilderment on Bob's face, and promptly responded, "I've got a book on leadership that I want you to read. It will help you to understand what I'm talking about. While it's written from a business perspective, I think you'll find it invaluable."

Pastor Bob took the book home with him. After supper, he read the first chapter before taking his son to play in the park as he had promised. The chapter defined vision. Now he knew what Jack meant by the term. He had misunderstood him. It was a leadership term more than a theological term, although they could overlap. Yes, it was a revelation for him but not necessarily the kind spoken of in the Bible. What did he learn? What is a vision in terms of leadership?

To understand our terminology and avoid miscommunication, it is time to define *vision* as used in these pages. Often in defining a concept it is helpful to examine what it is not before examining what it is.

What a Vision Is Not

Several terms have been used synonymously with but may not necessarily be the same as *vision*. One is *dream*. Dr. Martin Luther King, Jr. obviously used the terms equally in his famous "I Have a Dream" speech. I will also often use the terms as synonyms in this book, especially in the later chapters, for the purpose of variety.

While it may be used synonymously, in fact, a dream is much broader than a vision. The envisioning process most often begins with a dream. Dreams initiate or fuel visions. Indeed, most great visions are results of great dreams.

When helping leaders develop a vision, I often begin by asking them what they dream about. I ask, "What do you see in your mind when you think about your ministry in terms of the future?" If they see very little, I encourage them to set aside some time in their schedules on a regular basis to pray and seek God's direction regarding the future of their ministries. During this time they should dream about the future and answer questions such as, "If God would grant me one wish concerning my future ministry, what would it be?" This practice enhances the dream process.

Other terms often equated with visions are *goals* and *objectives*. There are several differences here. Goals and objectives are cold and abstract things which do not warm the heart. Vision, however, is warm and concrete and has the potential to melt the coldest heart. Just as a dream precedes a vision, so a vision precedes goals and objectives. Goals and objectives follow vision and are integral parts of the plan that ultimately brings about the realization of the vision.

A final term that is often confused with vision is *purpose*. At first glance the two appear indistinguishable, and this may be the case depending on their usage. However, there can be a subtle difference. Most often purpose answers the question, Why? Vision answers the question, What? Whether or not there is a difference depends on how a ministry answers these two questions. The reason a ministry exists may be the same as or different from what the ministry seeks to accomplish for Christ. Some argue that the purpose of the church is to glorify God, whereas the ministry of the church is the Great Commission. Others might wed the two.

What a Vision Is

I define an institutional vision as a clear and challenging picture of the future of a ministry as its leadership believes it can and must be.[1] This definition has five important facets.

It Is Clear

People cannot be expected to act on information they do not understand. To paraphrase the apostle Paul, if the bugle boy muffs the call to arms, what soldier will know to prepare himself for battle? (1 Cor. 14:8). While a well-developed vision statement has the potential to accomplish a number of important spiritual objectives, it accomplishes nothing unless it is clear and easily understood. If the people who make up the ministry do not or cannot understand the vision, then there is no vision regardless of the amount of time spent in developing it. The immediate goal is to brush away any mental cobwebs and vacuum any mental dust that might clutter the comprehension of the dream.

This raises the obvious question, How can you know if the dream is clear? A vision is clear when those who are a part of the ministry understand it well enough to articulate it to someone else. Therefore, it is wise periodically to quiz various individuals in general and the leadership in particular to determine their understanding of the vision. Ask them such questions as, "Where is this ministry going? What would you like to see this ministry accomplish? What do you think this work will have accomplished five years from now?" If people look puzzled or stammer and stutter, then your vision is obtuse and in need of clarity.

While all who are involved in the ministry have some responsibility to be involved in the process, clear vision casting is the primary responsibility of the point person or the primary leader of the ministry. First, the leader must be sure he has caught the correct vision from God. He must be sure that he understands what God desires for him. If there is a problem here, it is not God's fault, because God communicates clearly. The problem lies on the receiving end, with those who have not developed "ears to hear and eyes to see."

Next, leaders proceed to communicate that vision as clearly as possible so that their people understand what God's desire is for them. Moses is a case in point. He could not have missed God's vision for his people in Egypt. God spoke face to face with Moses when he declared his plan to liberate Israel from Egyptian bondage and lead them into "a good and spacious land, to a land flowing with milk and honey" (Exod. 3:8). The problem was with Moses' feelings of inadequacy to communicate the plan. Consequently, God instructed Moses to use Aaron as his "mouthpiece" until Moses was ready to assume the task (Exod. 4:16).

An example of clear vision casting is Nehemiah's message for the distressed remnant in Jerusalem, recorded in

Nehemiah 2. The directive is perfectly clear. According to verse 17, God's vision for them is to "rebuild the wall of Jerusalem." This statement has the decided advantage of being already concrete as opposed to others on a higher level of abstraction, such as Christ's vision for the church, the Great Commission. Of course, the rebuilding of the wall is symbolic of the more abstract vision of the restoration of Israel to a place where they glorify God and bring praise from all people for his name.

The goal of clarity is to discover the essence of the vision and present it in specific, concrete terms. Here the reward of such an approach is evident in the people's response as found in verse 18: "Then they said, 'Let us arise and build.' So they put their hands to the good work."

It Is Challenging

The problem for most ministry visions is that once they are conceived and born they face quick, untimely deaths and are quietly buried in some vision graveyard. If people are not challenged by the vision, there really is no vision.

I have worked with several ministries in developing a vision for their organizations. Most quit too soon. They begin the process with little idea of the time and energy necessary to develop a good vision. The result is a premature product that moves no one. Leaders must realize that if they themselves are not challenged by the final product, then the other people in the organization will not be challenged, either.

One problem is that it takes vision to develop vision. I suspect that in far too many cases a ministry organization realizes that it does not have a vision and desperately needs one. This is especially true of older, plateaued ministries. Originally they were the product of a visionary who has passed from the scene taking the vision with him. Lacking the first vision, an organization is not as motivated to develop a new vision in the same manner as when some early form or dream of the vision is already in place. The early form is the dream of what God wants the ministry to accomplish. This dream energizes and catalyzes the leadership and provides the staying power necessary to see the process through to the final product: a clear, challenging vision.

A second problem is that it is difficult for a group of people to develop a challenging vision. For example, finding a time when all of the leadership can meet together is next to impossible, especially in a church that works with busy laypeople. Also, when they do meet together, there is no guarantee that the creative juices will flow for them. The results of such meetings are more frustrating and discouraging than challenging, so that those involved are quick to quit.

Instead, it is best that the primary leaders of ministries be the pioneers who initially walk through the envisioning process. Presumably the point people are visionaries. Indeed, it is this visionary capacity that qualifies them to lead the organization in the first place. Once they have developed the vision, the next step is to present it in such a way that the leadership puts the team's "fingerprints" all over the vision so that they feel some personal ownership. It is at this point that the team is able to inject their insight and creativity into the process most efficiently and effectively. The result is that they become enthusiastic and are challenged by the final product. Then they, in turn, are ready to challenge others with the same.

It Is a Mental Picture

Vision is a "seeing" word. A good vision probes the imagination in such a way that it conjures up visual representations in the mind. John R. W. Stott says of vision, "It is an act of seeing—an imaginative perception of things, combining insight and foresight. . . . We see what it is—but do we see what could be?"[2]

Visionaries have the innate ability to see what others do not see. While they see needs, they have the natural capacity to see beyond those needs to the unique, exciting opportunities those needs present. For example, a nonvisionary person drives through urban or suburban America and sees apartments, houses, and men, women, and children. A visionary person drives through the same area and sees future ministries, possible meeting sites, even a potential congregation. No doubt Nehemiah carried a mental picture of the rebuilt gates with him from the time God gave him the vision until the gates were in place. Most likely Moses led the people of God in the wilderness with a picture in his mind of Israel living and serving God in a promised land "flowing with milk and honey." It is interesting to note that the end of Deuteronomy records that shortly before Moses' death, God took him up on Mount Nebo to show him the promised land (Deut. 34:1–4). This land was a vital component of God's promise and the ultimate realization of the vision (Exod. 3:8). While God had several purposes in mind for doing this, I suspect he wanted Moses to see the physical reality of what he had viewed and dreamed about mentally for all those years in the wilderness. It was God's physical, visible assurance to Moses that the dream was about to become a reality, even though Moses would not be a part of it.

It Is the Future of the Ministry

Vision is always cast in terms of the future. It is a mental picture of what tomorrow will look like. It is a view of a ministry's future and its exciting possibilities.

Visionary leaders spend a large proportion of time thinking about and living in the future. In doing so they largely determine their futures. By cultivating institutional visions leaders have a vital part in inventing and influencing the future of their ministries. They know precisely the kind of ministry they want and where they are going with that ministry and press on toward the accomplishment of their goals.

However, this does not mean that visionaries ignore either the present or the past. They often use the present as a platform to launch their ministries into the future. They may point to the status quo of the organization and use it to create dissatisfaction. Next they envision a better future and rally people to join them in moving toward it.

But how do visionaries relate to the past? Wise visionaries learn from the past, but their very nature will not allow them to live in the past. For them living in the past would be comparable to driving a car by looking through the rearview mirror. An example is the apostle Paul, who states: "But one thing I do: forgetting what lies behind and reaching forward to what lies ahead, I press on toward the goal" (Phil. 3:13–14).

Since the vision is the product of the visionary, it, too, by nature is futuristic. Some visions are short-term visions, but as long as they exist they concern the future. They are in a state of becoming, right up to the point of their accomplishment; then they are over and done with. This was the case with Nehemiah. Rebuilding the walls was his vision until they were in place. At that point the vision was accomplished and ended abruptly. The same is true of Moses' leading his people to the promised land and Noah's building the ark. These short-term visions were very concrete and not open-ended.

However, most visions are perpetually in the state of becoming and thus remain futuristic. These are long-term or open-ended visions. They are by nature broader, more abstract visions. An example is the Great Commission. The institutional vision of the church is the Great Commission, which includes pursuing, evangelizing, and discipling all people. While the church that pursues this vision will win people, hopefully lots of people, it will never fully accomplish the vision. In a very real sense, this is a paradox, for the church is successfully accomplishing that which cannot be accomplished.

In general, most ministry organizations plan for a relatively lengthy existence. However, a vision is the key to any long-term existence. Therefore, they need to develop broad, long-term visions that are perpetually in the state of becoming.

It Can Be

A good vision has potential. It rests firmly on the bedrock of reality, is highly feasible. The visionary leader possesses an uncanny sense of being on to something big for God, believing that God is planning something special and that the leader is a vital part of that plan.

Most often people and organizations err in one of two directions concerning the feasibility of a vision. On the one hand, there is little or no vision. Most are moving in this direction. While consulting with churches, I encounter this problem repeatedly. One of the major reasons 85 percent of the churches in America are either plateaued or dying is because they and their leadership have little or no vision. However, this is not a new problem. In Ephesians 3:20, Paul lightly slaps the Christians in Ephesus on the wrist for not thinking big enough when he says, "Now to Him who is able to do exceeding abundantly beyond all that we ask or think."

On the other hand, the vision may be too big. The problem here is twofold. Some people will not give the vision a fair hearing, because it is so vast that it tends to overwhelm them. They feel intimidated and defeated just listening to the vision. Others who initially pursue a vision that is too big later become disillusioned and discouraged with the ministry. There develops a sense of futility that eventually leads to a resignation from the ministry.

But how can you know when a vision is too big? This is difficult to determine, because most visions are not big enough. Also, Jesus repeatedly rebukes the disciples for their lack of faith, not the fact that their faith is too big. Three issues affect answering this question.

The first issue is, Who is the visionary; is he the right person to lead in accomplishing such a vision? People will question the visionary's character, credentials, and whether or not he is in the right position in the right organization to accomplish such a big vision. An example would be Bill Bright, whose vision for Campus Crusade for Christ is to win the world to Christ in this generation. Most give his vision high marks because of who he is and what God has accomplished thus far as the result of his vision.

The second issue is, Who are the visionary's people? It takes a big team to accomplish a big vision. Who is on the team? People will question their characters and capabilities to realize the vision. An example of a team with high credibility is the men and women in Campus Crusade who are so committed and highly motivated that they are willing to go anywhere to win the world for Christ.

The third issue is, Are the times right for this vision? Is there any evidence that the world in general or a group of people in particular is ready to come to Christ? One of the problems in American Christianity is that many leaders do not understand their times. For example, they have missed the shift in America from a churched to a nonchurched culture and the implications of this for their ministries. Consequently, their visions take on an appearance of unreality because they show they are unaware of the needs and values of today's vast nonchurched generation.

It Must Be

A good vision grabs hold and won't let go. Not only does the visionary believe that it can be, he is convinced that it must be. A critical sense of urgency dominates his thoughts. It might even keep him awake at night. He is so gripped by the vision that his spirit refuses to rest until the ministry is moving in the direction of the vision. Several variables contribute to this conviction.

One is the belief God is in it. He is the motivating force behind what the visionary wants to accomplish. There is little question that God has placed this vision on his heart. He has committed his life to accomplish God's will, and now God has revealed it in the form of the ministry dream. Nehemiah demonstrates this awareness of divine involvement when he says, "I did not tell anyone what my God was putting into my mind to do for Jerusalem" (Neh. 2:12).

A second variable is that God has chosen to accomplish this vision through this particular person. Perhaps God will use other leaders as well, but this person is convinced that

38

he will play a major role, just as God used King David to serve his divine purpose in David's generation (Acts 13:36). But how does a visionary person know this is the case? One indication is that God grants him success as he moves to accomplish God's will. Some have described this as God's opening the doors of opportunity. Nehemiah experienced this when King Artaxerxes granted his request to leave and go to Jerusalem to pursue his vision. The granting of this permission was so unlikely that Nehemiah knew God had to be in it. Perhaps this amazement is reflected in the fact that later he makes two references to it. In Nehemiah 2:8 he says, "And the king granted them to me because the good hand of my God was on me." Then in verse 18 he says, "The hand of my God had been favorable to me, and also about the king's words which he had spoken to me."

A third variable is that the vision will benefit people. A leader cares about people and is moved to believe that they will be better off because of it. In general, people will experience such benefits as eternal life, spiritual renewal, the healing of a marriage, reconciliation with a friend, and much more. And this only serves to excite and encourage the visionary even further. Dr. Martin Luther King, Jr. believed that his vision had to be, because it meant the freedom of black people in America from racism and oppression. Nehemiah reveals his heart for his people when he says in Nehemiah 2:17: "You see the bad situation we are in, that Jerusalem is desolate and its gates burned by fire. Come, let us rebuild the wall of Jerusalem that we may no longer be a reproach."

What have we learned so far? First, leaders should realize the importance of having a vision for their ministry organizations. Without a dream the ministry is in trouble. Second, they should arrive at a clear definition of institutional vision so that they know precisely what it is they are about and to avoid any misunderstanding or miscommunication. In the next chapter we will begin the creative process of developing a unique vision for a ministry.

Giving Birth: Part 1

Development of a Vision: The Participants

Pastor Bob could hardly wait to get home from the park. He felt sorry for his son, because he had not been very good company. Most of the time his mind was preoccupied with that book back on his desk in the house. He should not have read the first chapter before going to the park.

The excitement welling up inside him was pushing his discouragement aside. In addition, all kinds of ideas were flying around in his head. He jokingly thought, "Now I know how Columbus felt when he discovered America!" The first chapter alone had opened up a whole new world for him. It was the world of leadership in general and vision in particular. The concept of vision was most intriguing and offered some excellent insight into his leadership problems. He still had other questions, but for now, at least, he had some idea as to what his men were after. And it made lots of sense. "But what do I do now?" he asked himself. "How does one go about developing the vision?" And, just as important, "Who births the vision? Who is ultimately responsible?"

What Pastor Bob was about to learn was that birthing a vision has much in common with birthing a child. This would be easy to comprehend, because Bob and Mary were expecting their second child. Both events rely heavily on the personnel and the process. He knew that for birthing a child the personnel consisted of Mary, him, doctors, and nurses. The best process, according to their doctor, was natural childbirth. Before birthing a vision, he must ask two important questions: Who develops the vision, or who is involved in the envisioning process? and, How is the vision developed, or what is the envisioning process?

This chapter will answer the personnel question, the next chapter will deal with the process question. Who develops the vision? Initially ministry leaders are responsible for birthing ministry visions. Leaders must cultivate the vision, not followers. While good leaders listen to their followers, it is their role, not that of their followers, to collect and focus the information on a powerful, coherent ministry vision. But who are these leaders, and what is their role? In answering the first question I will discuss their position in the ministry organization, their number, and several important characteristics.

The Point People: Who Are They?

The ministry leader is the sole point person or the primary leader of the ministry. In the church, this person is the senior pastor such as Pastor Bob. In the parachurch, this individual goes by various titles such as president, general director, and so on.

A Single Leader

It is important to recognize that every ministry and every leadership team within a ministry needs a single leader. Today's emphasis on coleadership, especially in the church where it is known as lay elder rule, attempts to be biblical but most likely is an overreaction to leadership by a single tyrant or despot, or in some cases to weak or unskilled professional leadership. While the biblical foundation is suspect, the problem with coleadership is that people cannot follow a group. It is imperative that there be a single leader, or on a ministry team a leader of leaders.[1]

The general leadership principle here is that where two or more relate together as a team (whether as a family, ministry, or some other relationship) for any period of time, one must stand out as the leader or "head." Paul demonstrates this truth from a theological perspective in 1 Corinthians 11:3 where in a discussion of headship he says that "God is the head of Christ." The same idea is found in 1 Corinthians 3:23 and 15:28. The instructive principle to observe here is that even on the most perfect team in existence, the Trinity, there is headship. God the Father is the primary leader, the point person in the relationship.

From a practical perspective all the participants in a ministry or on a leadership team are not equal in their leadership abilities, knowledge, experience, reputation, training, and commitment. Some are born with natural gifts of leadership and later, in addition, may receive the spiritual gift of leadership (Rom. 12:8). Others have been blessed and gifted in other areas for ministry. It is important that those with special leadership gifts and abilities take positions of primary leadership in the various organizations.

A Visionary Leader

Not only is the vision developed initially by a sole point person, but this individual needs to be a visionary type person as well. It takes a visionary leader to cultivate a profound, positive vision of the future. What are the characteristics of these kinds of people? How would you know one if you saw one?

INTUITIVE. One characteristic which has surfaced among visionary leaders is a preference for relating to the world through intuition. Isabel Myers, one of the developers of the popular and widely used Myers-Briggs Type Indicator (MBTI), writes:

> Mankind is equipped with two distinct and sharply contrasting ways of perceiving. One means of perception is the familiar process of *sensing,* by which we become aware of

43

things directly through our five senses. The other is the process of *intuition,* which is indirect perception by way of the unconscious, incorporating ideas and associations that the unconscious tacks on to perceptions coming from outside. These unconscious contributions range from the merest masculine "hunch" or "woman's intuition" to the crowning examples of creative art or scientific discovery.[2]

When Myers refers to sensing and intuition she is discussing how people perceive or acquire information. She is referring to how we master finding out about things. She believes that people have the ability to use both processes, and do use both, but prefer to use one more than the other. For example, most people can use both their right and left hands but prefer to use one over the other when doing such things as writing or throwing. This she refers to as one's preference. People who prefer sensing acquire information through their eyes, ears, and other senses. They desire to discover what is actually there and is actually happening. These are the practical realists, the commonsense type of people in our world who focus on present reality.

However, people who prefer intuition gather information by looking beyond the senses to what some call a sixth sense. This "sixth sense" concerns the world of ideas, relationships, and possibilities which for the intuitive type person appear to flash out of nowhere. These people are future oriented and think not so much in terms of what is but what could be. They focus not on details and present realities but on the big picture and the exciting possibilities which lie in the future. In reviewing these characteristics, it becomes obvious that visionaries favor the intuitive over the sensing process.

It is important to note at this point that neither process is good or bad. Both are necessary to the ultimate success and survival of any ministry. Every ministry needs both types, and it is the role of the intuitive types to take the lead in developing the organization's vision with input from the sensing types of people. Isabel Myers estimated that about 75 percent of the population in America prefer the sensing process and 25 percent the intuitive process; however, samples collected by the professionals who administer and interpret the MBTI show that there are more intuitive type people in the population than reflected in Myers's estimate.[3]

People can discover whether they prefer the intuitive or sensor processes in several ways. One subjective but fairly reliable approach is to read the above descriptions of the two processes and determine which is most personally fitting. This assumes, of course, that a person has a good knowledge of how God has designed him or her. A more objective approach is to give these same descriptions to those who know the person well such as spouse or colleague and ask their opinion. A third way is to take the MBTI, which is an instrument designed to help a person determine the preferred sensing or intuitive process and the strength of each as well as other preferences.[4]

Naturally the question arises, Can a person who in the past has preferred the sensing process change to prefer the intuitive process and become more visionary? Isabel Myers and professionals who have worked with the MBTI believe that children are born into this world with a predisposition for one process or the other. This results in a preference for that process, which means that individuals will develop and trust the one more often than the other as daily they take in information from the world.[5] Consequently, persons who by design prefer the sensing process can develop their intuitive abilities, but only to a limited degree. By their very nature they are best at using the sensing processes. However, those who prefer the intuitive process can consciously develop and increase their abilities to use these functions and their visionary capacities to an even greater degree.

This raises the question, Who should be the primary leader in an organization, the sensing or intuitive type person? The natural tendency among people in the ministry organization, or the vision community, is to follow the more visionary or intuitive type leaders, because they have the unique ability to powerfully enable followers for ministry by communicating a unique, positive vision of the future. They display the strongest ownership of the vision. They best personify the vision and tend to be most dedicated to it personally. Consequently, the position of the point person or leader of leaders is best served by the developed intuitive type individual.

However, people who already are the primary leaders of a ministry organization may discover later that they prefer the sensing over the intuitive process. These leaders have two choices. One is to surround themselves with intuitive, visionary type people and rely heavily on their skills and abilities. The other choice is to step down from the point position and defer to someone else better equipped for this particular, unique role. This not only benefits the ministry but frees these individuals to pursue areas within or outside the ministry for which they are better designed. The result is a greater sense of accomplishment and fulfillment with minimal burnout.

INFORMATION COLLECTOR. In addition to intuition, another characteristic of visionary type people is their ability to recognize, collect, and synthesize pertinent information from a variety of sources. In short, they are great information collectors. One of my extremely gifted, visionary friends (who is in a high leadership position in a large ministry organization) has on several occasions with a big smile on his face referred to himself not as a pioneer but as a thief.

Jay Conger affirms this information-collecting role in *The Charismatic Leader* when he writes:

> I witnessed this same process among my own research subjects. The charismatic leaders were great information collectors with a difference—they used multiple and often apparently unrelated sources of information. Fred Smith says: "Mostly, I think, it is the ability to assimilate information from a lot of different disciplines all at once, particularly information about change, because from change comes opportunity. . . . The common trait of people who supposedly have vision is that they spend a lot of time reading and

gathering information, and then synthesize it until they come up with an idea."[6]

Essential to this information-collecting process is the information or knowledge gained from personal, hands-on experience. In their book *The Leadership Challenge* Kouzes and Posner indicate that intuition is the result of bringing together knowledge and experience. But this knowledge is not that which is gained in school but through hands-on experience in the marketplace. They conclude:

Direct experience with the organization and the industry is the source of knowledge on how the organization and industry operate. Intuition, insight, and vision come from the knowledge that we acquire through direct experience and store in our subconscious.[7]

Therefore, visionary leaders should seek and value any knowledge gained from their experience in ministry. There tends to be an emphasis in the American culture on knowledge gained from the classroom experience, especially in academic circles. The research which Kouzes and Posner cite above and elsewhere in their book indicates that knowledge gained from experience in the field contributes considerably more to the intuitive process. Thus, even when going to school, it is important that visionary leaders pursue involvement in some form of ministry because of the contribution this experience makes to that process.

In light of the importance of ministry experience, some people point to the fact that a number of pastors of the larger churches in America are not seminary trained people but individuals who came up through the ranks. I believe that, in general, this observation is correct. However, the key is to combine seminary training with good ministry experience in the field. Most reputable seminaries have field education programs that make provision for this during the leader's seminary years. The real danger is to value the classroom experience over field ministry experience, which is a common occupational hazard for seminarians.

Consequently, it is important that visionary leaders who desire to remain on the cutting edge of ministry regularly expose themselves to as many sources of information as possible. It is not merely a good idea for them to set aside time in their busy schedules for information collecting, it is a must. They must read lots of books and articles on leadership, change, and so on. They should also listen to tapes on the same and attend selected conferences put on by the various visionary, "hard-charging" churches and organizations across the land which God is blessing. And it is very important that they value past ministry experience and seek more of the same in the future. Actually, the ideal would be to pursue a year-long, full-time internship in a ministry that God is obviously blessing. The experience gained from such an internship would be invaluable. All of these sources will supply the visionary leader with a constant flow of raw data for the intuitive mind to digest.

A discussion of the role of intuition in leadership may give the impression that whole ministry visions and entire new ministry directions pop full blown into a visionary's mind at one sitting. In fact, this is rare. I believe that most visionaries combine the intuitive process in some fashion with the information-collecting process when envisioning the future of their ministries. The process of information collecting often supplies the raw data on both the conscious and subconscious levels, which the intuitive mind takes and uses to perceive new relationships, new ways of doing things, and potent possibilities for the future.

The Point Person: What Does He Do?

Numerous, unique ministry models exist which prescribe a leader's role in a particular Christian organization. While most attempt to be biblical, I suspect that other factors exert a strong influence on the leader's role or what he or she does in the point position. I am referring to such factors as the ministry community's expectations, the kind of ministry, the locale of the ministry, and so on. For example, a small church in the rural midwest expects its pastor to have strong people skills, for much of his ministry will take place in homes, hospitals, and nursing homes. However, a larger church in an urban or suburban community in the east might expect its pastor to display strong skills in the areas of communication and administration.

In answering the question, What does the visionary leader do? I would like to suggest what is for many a new paradigm. This paradigm involves the organizational leader in several functions.

Primary Communicator

The first function of the leader is to be primary communicator. In the parachurch, these are the leaders who represent the ministry to those on the outside. People look to them to discover what the ministry is all about and how it relates to them. Thus, they need to be articulate spokesmen for the organization. In the church, the primary communicators are the sole pastors or senior pastors who each Sunday are positioned behind the pulpit as prophets. It is their role to lead by communicating relevant, expository sermons from the Scriptures.

Developer of Leaders

A second function involves the development of both present and potential leaders for the ministry organization. This is an area which is much in neglect today, especially in the American church. Many pastors work hard at preaching but fail to develop leaders. A quick perusal of seminary catalogs reflects few, if any, courses that train people in leadership development whether in the classroom or the field.

However, no ministry will survive without leadership development. It will last only as long as the visionary leader is with the organization. When that person leaves, the ministry crumbles for lack of leadership.

But who is responsible for leadership development? It is the ministry leader's role to cultivate those at the top level of the organization's ministry team. Then, because they, too, are leaders, those on the ministry team develop, in turn, those who are under them at the lower leadership levels of the organization.

Vision Caster

A third function of leadership in this new paradigm relates directly to the envisioning process. I believe that the leader wears three hats in this capacity—those of vision cultivator, communicator, and clarifier.

VISION CULTIVATOR. The vision cultivator intuitively initiates and develops the organization's unique vision, which empowers the vision community for ministry.

VISION COMMUNICATOR. The vision communicator's function interfaces with the former function, for he is the primary communicator. Once the vision is cultivated and in place, the leader must keep it before the ministry community. Without the regular casting and recasting of the dream, people in the community are quick to stop dreaming and often behave as if there is no vision at all.

VISION CLARIFIER. Finally, the vision clarifier focuses the vision. Cutting-edge organizations are characterized by a whirlwind of activity and cataclysmic change. In the midst of this, there must be someone who regularly serves to rethink and further refine the dream. He helps people comprehend the vision and discover their part in it. He supplies precision answers as to how, when, and where those in the vision community can play a significant role in the realization of the dream.

This clarification means periodic rephrasing of the vision. It takes the same vision but looks for new, creative ways to express it as a means of infusing fresh life and power into the dream. An example of this process in the marketplace is McDonald's hamburger chain. One way they have chosen to express their vision is by developing slogans such as "Food, Folks, and Fun." However, these slogans are dynamic, not static in that they are changed once or twice a year in an attempt to catch the public's eye afresh and sell more products.

Finally, clarification helps to determine if it is time to rethink and possibly change the dream. Fred Smith argues that the mark of a good leader is to "know when it's time to change the vision."[8] He gives as an indicator the demographic changes that can take place in the community and the church. Other indicators might be a change in leadership and/or the purpose of the organization.

Nehemiah is a good example of a sole, visionary leader who was able to cultivate, cast, and clarify a vision for the people of God in his day. It is interesting to note that in this situation God raised up a single leader, not a group of coleaders who had no primary leader. People can follow only one visionary at a time. Nehemiah also appears to have been an intuitive collector of vital information as evidenced by his nightly inspection trips described in Nehemiah 2.

The text of Nehemiah does not give any details regarding the cultivation of the vision. It is possible that God gave him the vision directly, which would have considerably shortened the process. Nevertheless, Nehemiah was faithful in communicating and clarifying the dream, as he expressed it in chapter 2 when he appeared before both the king and the remnant in Jerusalem.

Significant Others

Birthing the vision begins with the visionary leader. Again, it takes a visionary to develop a vision. However, he cannot and must not do it alone. It is imperative that he involve others, "significant others," in the process. But who are these other people and what role do they play in the envisioning process?

Their Identification

These people whom I call the significant others are those who make up the leadership team. They are leaders and, therefore, significant people in the vision community. Fred Smith refers to them as "driving wheels" and declares their importance when he writes:

> There's a difference between people who provide the momentum in a group and those who go along for the ride. Wise leaders know that if they get the driving wheels committed, they will bring the others along. Without the commitment of the driving wheels, the organization moves unsteadily.[9]

Smith is correct. What is most important is that these leaders comprehend and fully commit themselves to the vision. They need to get their fingerprints all over the vision in order to gain comprehension and ultimately ownership of the vision. This is accomplished by including them in the envisioning process. When they feel as though they have been a part of the process, and their thoughts and ideas are accurately represented in the vision, then they are more apt to commit strongly to the vision.

Their Functions

The function of these significant others in birthing the vision is fourfold.

COOPERATION. First, they must cooperate with and follow the leadership of the visionary point person. It is imperative that they recognize his gifts and abilities in this area and trust his leadership in the process. They must avoid at all costs any power plays, special interests, and private agendas. These destructive practices have no place in the creation of a vision.

CONTRIBUTION. Second, these leaders must be a part of the process. The ability to aid in birthing the vision will vary from person to person depending on such factors as whether they are intuitive or sensing types and their other gifts and abilities from God. Obviously, some will make a greater contribution than others. It is most important that this be recognized, and that different individuals contribute in proportion to their abilities.

One area where these leaders may prove indispensable is in the supply of information that is vital to the formation of the dream. For instance, they may have a better grasp of the needs, values, and dreams of the ministry community than does the ministry leader. And often they are more familiar with the culture and demographics of the ministry area. Again, wise leaders listen to their people, especially to the significant others.

I would suggest that ministry leaders meet regularly with their leadership and gather as much information from them as time will permit. Some individuals may be given areas to investigate and research. In light of their time and their God-given abilities, ministry leaders will take this information and use their gifts to formulate the vision statement. Then they will take this back to the team and ask them to add to, change, or delete what the leaders have produced. A good vision statement will require few changes, and the team will feel ownership by virtue of having gone through the process.

SUPPORT. Third, the leadership team must rally in support of the vision. This involves far more than a simple vote in favor of the dream. They must get behind the effort. The kind of ownership needed at this point is enthusiastic support backed up by personal commitment as manifest through individual involvement. If leaders cannot support the vision, then they need to find a new ministry organization with a vision they can support.

COMMUNICATION. Finally, the significant others need to be involved in casting the vision. This is not the exclusive role of the ministry leader. The ministry community needs to hear the vision in many different ways from as many different sources as possible. One way a leadership team often serves the organization is by ministering in small groups to the individuals who make up the ministry community. This provides an ideal opportunity to communicate the dream to people on a more personal basis. The goal is that the ministry community also become the vision community, because the former becomes insipid without the latter.

So far we have looked at the primary participants who are a vital part of the envisioning process. Next, we turn our attention to the process itself.

Giving Birth: Part 2

Development of a Vision: The Process

Pastor Bob rushed into the house with his son close on his heels as the door slammed shut behind them. His little boy thought they were playing a game. But Bob could hardly wait to get back to that book. As he walked through the kitchen, he kissed his wife and headed straight for his desk in the spare bedroom. She smiled to herself, for it was not the first time she had seen this happen. But he had not seemed so intense the other times.

He devoured the next chapter and learned, just as he'd suspected, that the vision personnel consisted mostly of him as the ministry point person and his leaders as significant others. However, the major responsibility was on his shoulders, for he was supposed to be the primary leader on the team. Up until this time he had viewed himself mostly as a preacher of the Bible and a shepherd of his people, which meant that he spent much of his time in his study interpreting the text and developing sermons. What little time was left he spent visiting his people. He had never thought of himself as a vision caster. Why, it was not until recently that he had even heard of the word *vision* in terms of ministry and leadership.

Pastor Bob read on. He could not put the book down. Naturally, his next question was about the process of developing a vision. If he was responsible to develop the vision, then what was he supposed to do? How do you develop a vision? Is there a process? If so, what is it?

As already noted, birthing a vision has much in common with birthing a child. First, you must concern yourself with the right personnel. If you begin with the wrong vision personnel, chances are good that you will never make it to the vision process before the entire effort aborts. If you should make it that far, the child at best will suffer birth defects.

But it is not enough to have the right personnel in place. The process is critical to the product as well. The right people going through the wrong process spells disaster. The question to be answered is, How do you develop the vision; how can you custom-design a unique vision for your ministry? This chapter will answer the question by examining the vision birthing process, which consists of three stages, conception, development, and birth. It will conclude with a brief presentation and evaluation of several vision slogans.

The Conception of a Dream

The birth process, whether it involves a child or a vision, begins at conception. The conception stage of a vision has at least two crucial phases: initiation and expansion. The end result of this stage is a dream that eventually leads to the vision.

The Initiation Phase

The dream is most often initiated either by the dreamer's recognition of untapped opportunities or dissatisfaction with the status quo. Both provide fertile soil for the visionary mind.

UNTAPPED OPPORTUNITIES. Most visionaries are quick to recognize untapped opportunities. They have the uncanny ability to see things that other people miss. For instance, visionary leaders can drive through the inner city and see disciples where others see only poor lost people. They see places for potential Bible studies where others see only apartments. The apostle Paul was such a person. When he and Silas arrived in the city of Berea after a bad experience in Thessalonica, according to Acts 17:11, he was quick to recognize that the people in Berea were different from those in Thessalonica. The Bereans were people of integrity and were eager to know the Scriptures. This spelled opportunity for Paul, and he was quick to recognize and tap this opportunity by leading many of the Bereans to Christ, which was not possible in Thessalonica. Because the Bereans were willing to examine the Scriptures, the opportunity was there. However, certain Jews in Thessalonica were too antagonistic toward his ministry and were not interested in the Scriptures. There was no opportunity to tap.

DISSATISFACTION WITH THE STATUS QUO. Most often, however, a leader conceives a dream when he has a deep dissatisfaction with "what is" and a deep, pressing desire for "what could be." Few visionary leaders are satisfied with the status quo. For them maintaining the status quo equates maintaining ministry mediocrity. And mediocrity is a word not found in their dictionaries.

As a result, they are rather easy to spot in any organization. One obvious characteristic is that inevitably they will challenge the status quo in the organization. They quickly discover the organization's traditions, and begin to question them by periodically asking, "Why are we doing what we are doing?" Naturally, they find such unacceptable responses as, "We've always done it that way."

Obviously, this tendency to challenge "what is" can get them into trouble. On the one hand it can benefit a ministry by helping it to move forward; on the other hand it can alienate people in the process. Regardless of visionary leaders' approaches to challenging the status quo, whether gentle or too abrasive, they will encounter resistance along the way. Often people who are less visionary and used to long-standing traditions in their ministry organizations do not understand the visionary mind set. Challenging old ways means change, sometimes massive change, and that is the mentality of the visionary. Rather than see the potential benefits that change can bring to an organization, some feel threatened and may turn on the visionary leader.

Another way to spot these leaders is assessment. Self-assessment is particularly helpful for those who are considering future leadership or are early in the leadership process. Two tools that have proved most helpful in determining one's attitude toward the status quo are the *Personal Profile* and the *Biblical Personal Profile* produced by the Carlson Learning Company. These instruments are essentially the same, the difference being in the interpretive phase where the *Biblical Personal Profile* includes the temperaments of various biblical characters.

Both focus on four basic temperaments represented by the four letters *DISC*. The *D* stands for dominance, the *I* for influence, the *S* for steadiness, and the *C* for compliance. Those who fall under the first two temperaments (D and I) usually prefer to challenge the status quo, while those who fall under the last two (S and C) prefer to work with the status quo. However, we must also keep in mind that there are exceptions.[1] The final judge of one's own visionary capacities is the individual. However, these tools can be very helpful and may be obtained at minimal cost from most area counseling organizations or professional business consultants. The advantage of these tools is that they do not involve a lot of time and are self-interpretive, so do not require professional interpretation.

I have said that visionary leaders have much difficulty with the status quo. This is primarily because in almost every situation they have an unusual ability to see critical unmet needs, shortcomings, deficiencies in the system. Things appear to them as broken and in need of repair. They cringe when they hear, "If it ain't broke, don't fix it." To them, if you look hard enough, every organization, no matter how innovative or close to the cutting edge, has something in need of repair. There are no perfect people, and people make up ministry organizations; therefore, there are no perfect organizations.

Such was the case with Nehemiah. He had inquired of Hanani and those from Judah concerning the Jews there who had escaped the Babylonian captivity. When he heard that they were in "great distress and reproach" and the wall of Jerusalem was broken down (Neh. 1:2, 3), his heart was grieved, and he wept and mourned for days. Perhaps we can understand his grief best by realizing that Jerusalem was the place where God had chosen his name to dwell (Neh. 1:9). Yet this place was in a disastrous situation Nehemiah could not tolerate. What kind of testimony was this to Israel's pagan neighbors? What kind of testimony was this to Israel's God? Nehemiah would not rest until something was done to change it.

Martin Luther King, Jr., was both grieved and incensed by the general condition of black people in America. He realized that they, like the Jews in the Book of Exodus, were victims of oppression and racial injustice. And it was in this very oppressive context that he conceived his dream of dignity and respect for all blacks in a free America.

These examples are most instructive. First, you begin with a visionary leader such as a Nehemiah or a Martin Luther King, Jr. Next you add a visionary situation involving some need or deficiency. The result is a profound, significant dream for the future that has the potential to empower a people to bring about cataclysmic change.

The Expansion Phase

While the dream is initiated most often by a dissatisfaction with the status quo, it expands as a result of the desire for a viable alternative: what can and must be. This signals the expansion phase.

People other than visionaries may express deep dissatisfaction with what is. They, too, may be good at spotting critical unmet needs, inconsistencies, "flies in the ministry's ointment." The problem is that they are often the organization's "squeaky wheels," people within and sometimes outside the organization who constantly find fault.

The critics are most easily identified in two ways. First, many do not have any solutions for the problems they uncover and call attention to. They know something is wrong but not how to fix it. Second, there are some exceptions. There are "squeaky wheels" with solutions, but their solutions are characteristically out of touch with the ministry and its times. They are stalwarts of the status quo, and their ideas are heavily immersed in what is. I suspect that most of these people mean well, but ultimately they become more a part of the problem than a solution to the problem.

Visionary leaders are completely different from "squeaky wheels." The only thing they have in common is an awareness of the flaws. However, visionaries may be characterized as opportunistic. They possess a keen sense of strategic opportunity in the midst of adversity. They see solutions for unmet needs. They acknowledge and identify the problems, but often in the same breath offer viable, compelling ideas or solutions to those problems. These solutions are concepts that push beyond what is to what can and must be. These solutions in the form of ideas make up the dream, which, in turn, eventually solidifies into the vision.

But where do these solutions or ideas come from? Ultimately, the source is God. John Haggai writes:

> Any worthy vision comes from God, whether it deals with so-called "spiritual" matters or not—and whether the person with the vision is a Christian and realizes the source of the vision or not. Worthy visions are a gift of God. James said, "Every good gift and every perfect gift is from above, and comes down from the Father of lights, with whom there is no variation or shadow of turning" (James 1:17).[2]

The visions of Moses and Nehemiah had their sources in God. Moses writes that God supplied his dream from the midst of a burning bush (Exod. 3). Nehemiah acknowledged that his vision came from God, when he described his dream as "what my God was putting into my mind to do for Jerusalem" (Neh. 2:12). As one goes through the vision process, somewhere between the initiation and the expansion phases God implants the dream in the womb of the mind. This implantation of the dream, which ultimately leads to the vision, may take place directly or indirectly. The above examples illustrate a more direct process. However, Bennis and Nanus believe that the indirect process is more frequent.

> Historians tend to write about great leaders as if they possessed transcendent genius, as if they were capable of creating their visions and sense of destiny out of some mysterious inner source. Perhaps some do, but upon closer examination it usually turns out that the vision did not originate with the leader personally but rather from others.[3]

They cite several examples in support of this view, and then write the following:

> In all these cases, the leader may have been the one who chose the image from those available at the moment, articulated it, gave it form and legitimacy, and focused attention on it, but the leader only rarely was the one who conceived of the vision in the first place.[4]

In light of this, wise leaders must excel as readers and listeners and those who benefit from practical experience. In particular, they should read, listen to, and seek experience with those who think of new ideas, new images, and new paradigms. While God may directly implant the dream in the mind, more often he indirectly plants the information the leader collects from reading, listening, and practical experience as a dream in his subconscious mind. As visionary leaders view the shortcomings of a ministry and turn their attention toward a solution, this information intuitively comes from seemingly nowhere to form the embryo that develops into vision.

The Development of the Vision

During the development stage the dream moves closer to becoming a vision. There are several steps in the development stage.

Envisioning Prayer

The first step in development is the envisioning prayer. It may seem strange to bring up prayer at this point in the process. Should not the leader pray about the envisioning process much earlier than the development stage? The answer is yes. It is essential to bathe the entire process in prayer. However, sometimes leaders are not aware that they are in the conception stage. It happens before they know it. All they realize is that the ministry situation has unmet needs or provides unusual opportunity, and thoughts of solutions or exciting possibilities for those opportunities have begun to synthesize in their minds. While catalytic leaders constantly pray at any time in a broad, general way for vision, now they have something specific, a dream in particular, to pray about.

I call this envisioning prayer. It is not prayer for a ministry organization in general; rather, it specifically concerns the ministry vision. This prayer is for such specific things as vision wisdom and insight, the vision community, and visionary leadership.

This envisioning prayer is intentional. It must not be a haphazard, spur-of-the-moment kind of thing. Instead, visionary leaders often set aside regular times for envisioning prayer. They pray by themselves, with other leaders, and with those who make up the vision community. This sends to all others involved in the ministry process a clear message of the importance of the vision.

Jesus' own prayer life is instructive at this point. It would appear, according to Mark 1:35, that he practiced the discipline of awaking early in the morning and traveling to a solitary place where he could pray without interruption. While the text does not say how long Jesus prayed, I would suggest that visionary leaders also set aside an entire day once a month or once a quarter to get away early to a solitary place for a time of worship and prayer. It is imperative that this time include intentional prayer for and meditation over their personal and institutional visions.

As leaders practice intentional, envisioning prayer in combination with continued exposure to other visionary leaders, ideas will continue to pop into their minds and be added to their dreams. Apparently, this very process was taking place in Nehemiah's head as he prayed an envisioning prayer (Neh. 1:4–11). As soon as he heard about the desperate situation in Jerusalem, he fell to his knees in prayer. God brought the vision and possibly a strategy to implement that vision to his mind. At the end of his prayer he asked God to grant him success with Artaxerxes (v. 11). Nehemiah's prayer began with the situation in Jerusalem and finished with an initial strategy in place: to appear before King Artaxerxes. These acted as prayer "bookends," between which God gave Nehemiah his vision for the remnant in Jerusalem.

Thinking Big

The second step in the development of the vision is to think big. Small visions do not motivate. Someone has said, "Make no small plans, for they have not the power to stir the souls of men." Indeed, most successful vision statements are big-vision statements. Several examples throughout history bear this out.

Jesus Christ challenged a small band of disciples to reach the entire world with the gospel. When you examine the various texts on the Great Commission, you realize he was an individual of no small vision. He was a visionary par excellence.

In both Matthew 28:19 and Luke 24:47 Jesus designates whom the disciples are to reach with the gospel. They are commissioned to pursue not just a few Palestinian locals but the nations. Specifically, in Matthew 28:19 they are told to "make disciples of all the nations." In Luke 24:47 they are to preach repentance for the forgiveness of sins to "all the nations."

In Mark 16:15 and Acts 1:8 Jesus determines where the disciples are to go with the gospel. They are to go into "all the world," and they are to witness not only in their immediate community but "in Jerusalem, and in all Judea and Samaria, and even to the remotest part of the earth."

The size of his vision is even more amazing in light of the twelve men whom he chose to accomplish the vision. Peter, Andrew, James, and John were local professional fishermen. Matthew was a despised tax collector. Why did the Savior choose them? How could a few provincial locals catch the vision for the entire world? Had they ever ventured to think outside the confines of their own community? Before it was all over, the twelve had been reduced to eleven with the attrition of Judas. Yet this did not daunt the Savior, and after he returned to the Father these same men caught and began the task of implementing his dream, which has spread across the world. In fact, you and I would not be Christians today if it had not been for them.

In his doxology in Ephesians 3:20 Paul challenges the Christian community at Ephesus and all who make up the church of Jesus Christ to pray and think big. In verse 14 Paul concludes the first three chapters of the book with a doxology that stretches to verse 21. In verse 20 he states, "Now to Him who is able to do exceeding abundantly beyond all that we ask or think, according to the power that works within us. . . . " This says that our God is able to do far more than we ask or think, with the subtle implication that we do not ask or think big enough. In the rest of the passage Paul explains that God accomplishes these things not through us but through the power that works within us, which is a reference to the Holy Spirit (v. 16).

I find it interesting that even as far back as the first century A.D. God's community of faith had to be challenged or at least reminded to pray and think big. But this is critical if a ministry community is to be transformed into a vision community. I have observed that most people who make up a ministry community tend not to think beyond their own immediate world. Perhaps they become too caught up in the mundane affairs of everyday life. But in contrast, God seems to expect that which appears to most people to be impossible. Consequently, God raises up visionary leaders like Paul to challenge them and us to think big, because we have a big God who is more than able to accomplish big things through us in this big world.

Martin Luther dared to dream big dreams for God. He came to faith in Jesus Christ while a priest in the Roman Catholic Church. In light of his conversion and in contrast to the teachings of the church he began to see the need for other viable, biblical teachings. The only problem was that in those days there was no alternative. The Catholic Church was considered to be the only teacher of one biblical truth. To consider something else was heresy and was to risk his life. Yet his vision drove him on, and God used it to help fuel the Reformation.

Henry Ford had an incredibly large dream. He envisioned an affordable automobile for every family at a time when automobiles were only luxurious novelties. The average person traveled by foot, horse, train, or boat. People in his day were at first skeptical of his dream, but Ford's development of the assembly line and mass production of automobiles changed forever world manufacturing and the American way of life.

Martin Luther King, Jr., envisioned not just his own freedom but that of all black Americans. He was born and raised at a time in America when whites considered blacks to be inferior and denied them among other things their civil rights. Nevertheless, dauntless and at risk to his own life, he moved forward inspired by Moses in the Old Testament, and before his assassination he saw the partial realization of his dream.

But how can the dreamer know if his vision is big enough? Several factors can help in assessing the size of the vision. First, the vision has to be bigger than the envisioner in the sense that it goes far beyond him and his abilities to accomplish it. If he feels that it is within his grasp to accomplish the vision, then it is probably too small and limits God. When Christians develop visions that go beyond their abilities, they are forced to bring God into the picture and begin to trust him to play the major role in realizing the vision. When this happens, in a sense, the sky becomes the limit.

Second, if the dreamer's vision is too small, his people will not feel challenged. Most people delight in being stretched in their thinking, especially in terms of their future. In general, small visions do not stretch people and challenge them to action. On the other hand, if the vision should be too large, the result is discouragement. People will not view such a vision as realistic and will become frustrated and unproductive; some will drop out of the ministry.

Third, the natural tendency for most Christians is to think too small. This is Paul's point in Ephesians 3:20. The visionary leader's attitude toward risk taking may be helpful here. He needs to carefully scrutinize himself and determine if he tends to be a risk taker or not. If he does not like to take risks, then either his vision is too small and he should try to double or triple the size of his dream, or he may decide the role of visionary leader does not suit him after all.

Fourth, he needs to ask, How big is my God? Most often, the size of a person's vision reflects the size of his God. People who have a big view of God have a big vision. They see him as able to accomplish big things because he is such a big God. And, of course, the opposite is true as well. People who have a small God have small visions. They do not see him accomplishing great things, because they have missed who he is. Here, interestingly, their vision serves as a barometer of their doctrine of God.

Suppose a person discovers that his vision is too small. How might he grow a bigger vision? How does he increase the size of his vision? One way is to pray and ask God to increase his faith and consequently his vision (Mark 9:23, 24). Second, he can surround himself with people who think big, and expose himself to visionaries by reading their books and articles and by listening to their tapes. I would include some marketplace visionaries as well, such as Lee Iacocca, Ross Perot, Mary Kay Ash, Steven Jobs, Joel Arthur Barker, and others.

Another way to expand vision is to think strategically. Perhaps an illustration from my own life will prove helpful. A careful study of Paul's church-planting trips in the Book of Acts reveals that he and his teams did not go just anywhere but targeted strategic cities in Asia Minor, Greece, and Macedonia. Consequently, I train my potential church planters at Dallas Seminary to target strategic cities in America and abroad. For example, if I should plant a church in Dallas, I would target the Dallas metroplex, not just one of its many communities. My strategy would be first to plant a church in a fast growing suburban community of Dallas. Then, as the church grew, I would use it as a model and base of operations to launch other church plants in other suburban areas, the inner city, and some rural areas. I would challenge the people in these churches to target their places of work for Jesus Christ. For instance, those who work in some of the large buildings downtown could claim those buildings for the gospel. They could start prayer groups for those who are believers and evangelistic Bible studies during the lunch hour to reach those who are not.

While we might not be able to reach every person in the Dallas metroplex, our presence would be felt in the city community. If God accomplished this through Paul and his teams in Corinth, Ephesus, Berea, and other cities, why could he not accomplish the same through us in Dallas?

Written Brainstorming

As the dreamer prays envisioning prayers and thinks big, the next step is to begin writing his thoughts down on paper, recording the dream. I call this written brainstorming: putting on paper what God is putting on your heart. Here two important things take place: the collecting and recording of the contents of the dream.

This has several advantages. As God brings envisioning ideas to mind, they need to be put on paper before they are forgotten. Often, the mind works in such a way that thoughts surface in rapid-fire succession. At other times, a brilliant idea comes from nowhere while a person drives down an expressway or watches the evening news. Whatever the situation, there is no guarantee that he will be able to recall that information later. The only wise recourse is to put this material down on paper or into a portable tape recorder when it occurs.

Another advantage is that it forces a person to be disciplined in his thinking as he works through the envisioning process. He should set aside regular times in his schedule to sift through his spontaneous ideas and develop the dream into the vision. He may also spend time to think progressively and logically through the contents he finds in other good vision statements as long as they do not inhibit or limit or sidetrack his own dream.

Writing also forces him to be specific. I describe this as "blowing the lint off the brain." The point is this: If an idea cannot be written down, then it is far too general and vague and needs to be refined to the point where it can be. Even then, what is first put on paper will necessarily be broad and general, but it may contain some specifics as well. The writing process captures a necessary broadness that works in tandem with a certain narrowness, both of which are necessary to arrive at a clear vision.

In written brainstorming, just as in verbal brainstorming, it is important to record all thoughts no matter how unimportant they may seem. Decisions as to their importance will be made later in the process. This is not the point at which to evaluate the information, only to collect and record it.

This means writing as many pages as necessary to record all the information that is a part of the dream. These pages may be either few or numerous. The initial intuitive ideas God brings to mind will lead to a certain amount of necessary research at some point. For example, God brings to mind a particular people group as a part of the vision. This will necessitate some research into the demographics and psychographics of these people, and a certain amount of this information will need to be recorded for purposes of focus.

Organizing the Material

While a creative person never ceases to brainstorm, he does reach the time to organize the collected information, the fourth step in the development of the vision. This provides a skeleton later to be fleshed out with more information.

The "bones" of the skeleton are the contents found in good vision statements. But what are the contents of a good vision statement? A survey of vision statements indicates that the contents often vary even among similar ministries such as churches. Since there are no rules that govern what may or may not go into a vision statement, this variety can be healthy; each statement reflects what is unique about a particular ministry in relation to other similar organizations.

In general, vision statements include such information as the ministry's purpose, values, strategy, people, place, and finances. Some vision statements include only one or two of these; others may include them all.

STATEMENT OF PURPOSE. Practically every vision document contains a statement of purpose. This tells why the ministry exists or what it hopes to accomplish. People need and want to know this. Therefore, it is essential that those who are involved in a ministry or desire to plant a ministry (church planting or parachurch planting) think through and determine the purpose of that ministry. They ask and answer, Why are we doing what we are doing? This seems so basic that one might wonder why it should even be mentioned here. Yet in asking those involved in various ministries the *why* question, I have found that far too many do not have an answer, or they answer with great difficulty.

I believe that the problem here is twofold. On the one hand, people in some ministries cannot answer the question because the ministry does not have a vision. On the other hand, some cannot answer the question because, while the ministry has cultivated a vision, it has not clearly articulated and cast the vision. Here the difficulty lies not so much with the vision but with the communication of the vision. The purposes of parachurches will vary among the different organizations. Usually they are subsumed in some way under the Great Commission. For example, the purpose of Dallas Theological Seminary, where I teach, is the preparation of men and women for ministry in the Great Commission, as expressed in its mission statement:

> Dallas Theological Seminary's mission as a professional, graduate-level school is to prepare men and women for ministry as godly servant-leaders in the body of Christ worldwide. By blending instruction in the Scriptures from our doctrinal perspective with training in ministry skills, the seminary seeks to produce graduates who do the work of evangelism, edify believers, and equip others by proclaiming and applying God's Word in the power of the Holy Spirit.[5]

Another example is Campus Crusade. Bill Bright's stated purpose for this parachurch ministry is found in the following quotation: "At this time and in a very definite way, God commanded me to invest my life in helping fulfill the Great Commission in this generation. I was to begin by helping to win and disciple the students of the world for Christ."[6]

The purpose of the church is the Great Commission, that is, making disciples of all the nations (Matt. 28:18–20; Mark 16:15; Luke 26:46–47; Acts 1:8). Consequently, the vision statement of the church should creatively reflect the Great Commission. But what, more precisely, is the Great Commission? What does discipling the nations involve? Many churches wisely divide the Commission into two parts consisting of evangelism and edification but emphasize one at the expense of the other. I have a different view, which affects how churches and ministry organizations should try to implement the Commission in our culture in the future. According to Matthew 28:19, 20 and Mark 16:15, three components make up the Commission and unfold chronologically.

The first is the intentional pursuit of lost people. This is reflected in the word *go* found at the beginning of the Commission in both Matthew 28:19 and Mark 16:15. The Savior clarifies what he means by this term in Luke 19:10 where he says, "For the Son of Man has come to seek and to save that which is lost." It is important to note that the infinitive *to save* is preceded by the infinitive *to seek*. The reason, as reflected in the context (Luke 19:1–10), is that the Savior's mission was first to seek out or pursue lost people and then to save them. In the context are two sections, a seeking section where the Savior pursued Zaccheus (vv. 1–7), and a saving section where he saved the diminutive tax collector (vv. 8, 9).

This concept of pursuing or seeking that which is lost is also found in the parables in Luke 15 (as well as other portions of Luke's Gospel). The Pharisees and the scribes were complaining (vv. 1, 2) because the Savior ate with "sinners." Eating with sinners was something that no self-respecting, religious Jew would have done, especially a rabbi. Jesus explains his behavior by telling a parable about a man who pursued a lost sheep and a woman who sought a lost coin. Just as both a sheep and a coin have value, sinners have value to God and are worth intense pursuit.

What is novel about these passages of Scripture is that in each case Christ intentionally targets and seeks the nonreligious crowd, those who were the nontempled people of his day. Within the past thirty years, America has experienced a shift from what was in the 1950s a churched culture to what at the end of the twentieth century is largely a nonchurched culture. George Gallup writes: "The evidence is that the churches have not made any inroads into attracting the unchurched over the past decade: in 1978, 41 percent of all American adults (18 or older) were unchurched; in 1988, that figure rose to 44 percent."[7] Concerning church attendance by the year 2000, Barna writes:

> Church attendance on Sunday mornings will decrease to about 35 percent of the population on any given weekend. This figure would drop lower if it were not for the growing body of congregations that will change the long-standing pattern and offer worship services on Saturdays, and on Sunday afternoons, in addition to (or, occasionally, instead of) the traditional Sunday morning time.[8]

Before the culture shifted in its attitude toward the church, much evangelism took place within the walls of the facility on Sunday morning, because most people, whether sincere in their Christianity or not, went to church on Sunday. However, today that custom has changed, and the evangelical church will not survive unless it intentionally and aggressively pursues nonchurched people. The days have long since passed when the church could sit back and wait for people to come to it. More and more are interested in doing other things on Sunday. Instead, the church must go to them.

Occasionally some unchurched will come back for a visit, especially when they marry or have a child. Gallup refers to this as the "life cycle effect" and explains that young people often leave the church either in their late teens or early twenties but may return in their late twenties.[9] It is important that when they return they find a church which holds strongly to orthodox Christianity but maintains a culturally relevant methodology.

The second component of the Great Commission is evangelism. In Mark 16:15 Christ says, "Go into all the world and preach the gospel to all creation." A Great Commission church places a high priority on evangelism. The church in general and the people in particular not only actively seek lost people, they reach lost people.

Church growth experts indicate that a church can experience growth in one of three ways: biological, transfer, or conversion growth. Biological growth occurs when churched people have children who grow up in the church, eventually accept Christ, and continue as church members. Transfer growth takes place when people leave one church and move to another. This method of growth may or may not be beneficial depending on people's reasons for leaving their former churches. A Great Commission church grows not because it emphasizes biological or transfer growth but because of its emphasis on conversion growth. Indeed, a church that does not reach the unconverted has lost its purpose.

The third component of the Great Commission is edification. Once the church reaches people it does not drop them but proceeds to enfold and disciple them. This is the process of edification, which brings new believers to a Christ-like loving demeanor and lifestyle that is taught and strengthened through a combination of such critical areas as Bible study, fellowship, communion, and prayer (Eph. 4:11–16; Acts 2:42).

But how might the purpose statement actually be expressed in a vision statement? What would it look like? Pastor David Stevens, who planted Lakeview Community Church in Cedar Hill, Texas (a suburb of Dallas), has developed an excellent vision statement. In it he includes the following statement of purpose:

> Our comprehensive purpose is to honor our Lord and Savior, Jesus Christ, by carrying out his command to make disciples of all nations (Matthew 28:18–20). Specifically, we believe God has called us to focus on reaching those in Cedar Hill and the surrounding area who do not regularly attend any church.[10]

This purpose statement contains several key components. First, it identifies the broad purpose of Lakeview as that of honoring Christ. This is followed by a general strategy for accomplishing it, which is the Great Commission exhortation to disciple the nations. Finally, it focuses the Commission on the nonchurched in Cedar Hill and the surrounding area.

STATEMENT OF VALUES. In addition to a statement of purpose, many vision statements include the ministries' values. They clarify what is unique and different about those particular ministries from other similar ministries. They also show what the ministries will emphasize and by omission what they will not emphasize. Some of these values are biblical absolutes while others find their source in biblical truth. Value statements for churches include such important items as commitment to the Scriptures as God's truth, relevant Bible preaching and teaching, excellence in leadership and ministry, relevant evangelism, ministry in small groups, an emphasis on prayer, authentic and contemporary worship, lay assessment and involvement, and so on.

Pastor Stevens also includes the following list of values in his vision statement:

A Commitment to Relevant Bible Exposition. We believe that the Bible is God's inspired Word, the authoritative and trustworthy rule of faith and practice for Christians. The Bible is both timeless and timely, relevant to the common needs of all people at all times and to the specific problems of contemporary living. Therefore, we are committed to equipping Christians, through the preaching and teaching of God's Word, to follow Christ in every sphere of life.

A Commitment to Prayer. We believe that God desires his people to pray, and that he hears and answers prayer (Matt. 7:7–11; James 5:13–18). Therefore, the ministries and activities of this church will be characterized by a reliance on prayer in their conception, planning, and execution.

A Commitment to Lay Ministry. We believe that the primary responsibility of the pastor(s) and teachers in the local church is to "prepare God's people for works of service"

(Eph. 4:12). Therefore, the ministry of Lakeview Community Church will be placed as much as possible in the hands of nonvocational workers. This will be accomplished through training opportunities and through practices which encourage lay initiation, leadership, responsibility, and authority in the various ministries of the church.

A Commitment to Small Groups. We are committed to small group ministry as one of the most effective means of building relationships, stimulating spiritual growth, and developing leaders.

An Appreciation for Creativity and Innovation. In today's rapidly changing world, forms and methods must be continually evaluated, and if necessary, altered to fit new conditions. While proven techniques should not be discarded at whim, we encourage creativity and innovation, flexibility and adaptability. We are more concerned with effectiveness in ministry than with adherence to tradition.

A Commitment to Excellence. We believe that the God of our salvation deserves the best we have to offer. The Lord himself is a God of excellence, as shown by the beauty of creation; further, he gave the best that he had, his only son, for us (Rom. 8:32). Paul exhorts servants, in whatever they do, to "work at it with all your heart, as working for the Lord, not for men" (Col. 3:23). Therefore, in the ministries and activities of Lakeview Community Church we will seek to maintain a high standard of excellence to the glory of God. This will be achieved when every person is exercising his or her God-given spiritual gift to the best of his or her ability (1 Cor. 12).

A Commitment to Growth. Although numerical growth is not necessarily a sign of God's blessing, and is not a sufficient goal in itself, we believe that God desires for us to reach as many people as possible with the life-changing message of Jesus Christ. Therefore, we will pursue methods and policies which will facilitate numerical growth, without compromising in any way our integrity or our commitment to Biblical truth.

There are several noteworthy characteristics in this value statement of Lakeview Community Church. First, it begins in the form of expressed commitments, not just statements of fact. The term *commitment* is meant to be a strong term as used here, for these are things that go beyond mere belief. The church not only adheres to them but has made the strongest of commitments to them. They will constantly be emphasized and valued throughout the life and ministry of the church.

These expressed commitments are then followed by a statement of values, which are explained briefly without a lot of detail. Often they are accompanied with appropriate scriptural references and further clarification. For example, in the commitment to growth is the additional clarification that the church is not simply interested in numbers for numbers' sake but as an indication of its desire to reach nonchurched people.

Finally, the conclusion of each value statement is accomplished in one or two sentences preceded by the word *therefore*. They summarize the value and may show how the value will be accomplished or practically applied to the ministry community.

Some vision statements also contain a doctrinal statement. I mention it here because I would include this as a part of the values of the ministry. In the evangelical community in particular, people want to know what you believe about God, the Scriptures, Jesus Christ, salvation, and other important doctrines of the Bible. Therefore, its inclusion can be helpful in attracting those of similar beliefs and deterring those who differ. Finally, the doctrinal statement should be brief and include only that which the ministry feels is essential to its faith and practice.

STATEMENT OF STRATEGY. A third component found in some vision statements is the strategy the ministry will implement to accomplish its purpose. Again, Lakeview Community Church's vision statement contains a noteworthy strategy. I have included it here with the purpose statement to show how the two may come together in the vision statement. It is preceded by the words *"In order to accomplish this."*

> Our comprehensive purpose is to honor our Lord and Savior, Jesus Christ, by carrying out his command to make disciples of all nations (Matt. 28:18–20). Specifically, we believe God has called us to focus on reaching those in Cedar Hill and the surrounding areas who do not regularly attend any church. In order to accomplish this, Lakeview Community Church will be an equipping center where every Christian can be developed to his or her full potential for ministry. This development will come through:
>
> a) creative, inspiring worship;
> b) teaching which is Biblical and relevant to life;
> c) vital, supportive fellowship; and
> d) opportunities for outreach into the community in service and evangelism.

This strategy statement has several exemplary features. First, it refers to the church as an equipping center. This is a first-century concept found in Ephesians 4:11. It is the idea that the church is not only a place of ministry but a base of ministry. However, Stevens has clothed it in fresh, descriptive language that appeals to the modern mind.

Next, it touches the felt needs of today's Christians by affirming that it seeks their personal development. Some nonchurched people caricaturize today's churches as spiritual "leeches." They complain that churches have a tendency under the guise of spiritual service to suck all the life out of a person without giving much in return—their excuse for not attending. This statement says you get something in return for being a part of the Lakeview community. There is value in becoming a part of them. Their desire is to help members achieve their full potential for ministry in Christ.

Finally, the specifics of the strategy are worship, teaching, fellowship, and evangelism. But this is not just any kind of worship; it is "creative, inspiring worship" that, based on Scripture, promises to relate to life as lived from Monday through Sunday. Life has a way of "beating up" on people, and this church says that the Bible has something to say about surviving those bouts. The fellowship is more than coffee and doughnuts before the service. Instead, it supplies vital relationships that support people who are at various stages in life. Finally, the church seeks to penetrate its community by serving the community rather than expecting the community to serve it.

STATEMENT REGARDING PEOPLE. Some vision statements include a reference to people, often the people who make up the ministry team. In this case, they are included for purposes of identification and ministry credibility. An important question that some will ask is, What qualifies these people to lead this ministry? Therefore, the document may include such information as each individual's age, family, education, prior ministry experience, awards, special talents and abilities, and other relevant data. It may be expressed in as little as a few sentences or as much as an entire page.

These people may also be those who make up the ministry's target group. A natural question is, Whom are you attempting to reach? Lakeview Community Church has targeted those "who do not regularly attend any church." Campus Crusade envisions reaching the students of the world. Dallas Seminary has targeted men and women who desire to be leaders at home and abroad.

STATEMENT OF THE PLACE OF MINISTRY. A fifth component found in some vision statements is information concerning the place of ministry. The question here is, Where will the purpose statement be realized? Most answer the question by describing their target area. This may be the immediate community. Again, Lakeview Community Church is representative: "Specifically, we believe God has called us to focus on reaching those in Cedar Hill and the surrounding areas who do not regularly attend any church." The target area may include the whole world. Lakeview Community adds: "We further intend to multiply our world-wide ministry by planting churches, by preparing our people for leadership roles in vocational ministries and parachurch groups, by sending out missionaries, and by becoming a resource center and model for Texas and the nation."

In describing the place of ministry, some vision statements will cover a modest amount of demographic material. This often includes the various elements that make up a community profile, one of which is statistics on the community's population such as how many people live in the area and whether it is declining or attracting new growth.

Another element concerns community housing. What is the dominant housing type, single family or multifamily? What are the values of existing houses and what kind of housing is projected for the future?

A third element focuses on education. Does the area have a high or low level of educational achievement? How many years of education has the average adult completed? What are the plans for future educational development?

A fourth element is occupation. What do the people in the community do for a living? Who is the primary employer? Are the people in white- or blue-collar occupations?

A final element is household income. What is the average household income? Is this above or below the national average? Are most people clustered together, or are there extremes?

STATEMENT OF FINANCES. A few ministry visions address finances, most often in statements for new ministry starts, especially those that depend on business loans or raising outside support. These costs are communicated on paper in the form of proposed personal or ministry budgets.

Again, it should be kept in mind that the majority of vision statements do not contain all of the above material. The contents are affected by the nature of the ministry. As leaders tailor their vision statements for their particular ministries, the necessary contents will become obvious.

Questioning the Dream

A fourth step in developing the vision is to probe the dream with constant questions. While there is no limit to the questions one can ask, here are a few musts. First, is the dream clear? Can others understand it? People cannot be expected to accomplish what they do not understand. In fact, if people do not understand the vision, then, in effect, there is no vision. Obviously the best determiner is to invite others to peruse the vision document for its clarity. Ask them to explain the vision based on what is written. This adds an eye-opening objective element to what otherwise can be a subjectively blind process.

Second, is the dream challenging? When people in the ministry community hear the dream, are they inspired? Often the problem with some visions is that they merely perpetuate more of the same old thing. They merely propel the status quo into the future. The statement sounds something like, "If it ain't broke, don't fix it!" The problem is that the status quo challenges no one. Visionary leaders understand this and think, But it is broke, so let's fix it anyway. However, while challenging vision statements may propose something that few have ever done before, most give a new, more relevant twist to an old idea. Consequently, they often transform the way things have always been done, which has an invigorating and inspiring effect on the vision audience.

Third, is the dream visual? Good visions create mental pictures. People must be able to see what the leaders see. In his book *Hey, Wait a Minute* John Madden asks Vince Lombardi about the differences between good and bad coaches. Lombardi answers, "The best coaches know what the end result looks like, whether it's an offensive play, a defensive play, a defensive coverage, or just some idea of the organization. If you don't know what the end result is supposed to look like, you can't get there."[11] The same holds true for leaders and their followers. Consequently, a critical question in the envisioning process is, What do you see?

Fourth, is the dream future oriented? Vision statements are statements about the future. Not only do they create mental pictures, but they are pictures of tomorrow and what tomorrow looks like. Visions learn from the past but do not live in the past. Actually, they serve as bridges from the past into the future. Therefore, dreams are preoccupied with the future and serve to project people into that future. Therefore, the question to ask is, Is this dream preoccupied with yesterday, a rehash of the "same old same old," or is it focused on tomorrow and the exciting possibilities tomorrow holds?

Fifth, is the dream realistic yet stretching? This is one of the more difficult questions to answer. In a very real sense, the visionary walks a tightrope attempting to balance challenge with reality. On the one hand the dream must be big enough to inspire people to action while on the other hand realistic enough so as to maintain credibility. An example of an unrealistic vision would be the challenge to reach thousands of people in either a small, sparsely inhabited rural community in midwest America or a Muslim community in another land.

Finally, is the dream culturally relevant? The answer to this question calls for a re-examination of the people in the ministry's target group. The key here is to communicate the dream to people, especially those of another culture, in ways they can understand. Walk the dream through the ministry personnel or the potential target community. Does it propose solutions for the people's legitimate felt needs? Does it take into consideration what they value and deem important? Does it incorporate language that is understandable and socially acceptable?

Demonstrating Patience

A fifth vision development step is giving the process enough time. Do not rush it. The dream must be carefully wrapped in the foil of creativity and baked slowly, often very slowly, in the oven of time. In short, be patient.

It is true that some visions pop full blown into a leader's head within a very short period of time. This seemed to be the case in the Old Testament with Nehemiah who, according to Nehemiah 1, received his vision in a matter of days (v. 4). While the chronology of the text is not entirely clear, Nehemiah was praying an envisioning prayer of confession and petition for his people when, apparently, God provided the vision. At the close of his prayer (v. 11) he indicates that he has God's vision for his people, the Jews in captivity, because he asks for success as he approaches King Artaxerxes with that vision.

However, my experience with seminarians and those in vocational church and parachurch ministry is that this is the exception rather than the norm. Most visions are made up of bits and pieces collected from various sources over a significant period of time. Add to this the fact that dreams work very closely with creativity, which cannot be rushed. Most often they may be several years cooking on the back burner of the visionary's mind. Then, when the time is right, they happen.

But how much time is necessary to develop a significant vision? The answer to that one is easy: whatever time it takes. If a leader is cultivating a vision and nothing much has happened, then it is obvious he has not given it sufficient time. I am aware of one visionary pastor who developed his ministry vision over one summer. For others it takes much longer.

I have discovered from my experience working with ministry organizations that the fatal flaw in attempting to formulate a vision is the tendency to rush the process. This is especially true of churches who work with dedicated volunteers. The problem is that a group of members, most often a board, are only able to carve out a weekend from their busy schedules to walk through the process. The result is that they never leave the starting block or that they dash through the process. In either case, little is accomplished, and they become extremely frustrated over what they feel is a waste of their valuable time. In some situations they may produce a vision document, but most likely it is insipid and empowers no one. The result is a general loss of enthusiasm for developing a vision even among those who know better.

A much wiser approach is to place in the point position an empowered, visionary leader who has already walked through the envisioning process and has a significant dream for the ministry's future. The meetings with this leader are more for the purpose of articulating than for mutually cultivating the dream from the very beginning. It may be that others, when they hear the dream, will add wisdom and insight. In this case, it is important that they do so for the purpose of acquiring ownership of the dream. However, most will recognize a good dream and may not add a lot to it. The result of these kinds of limited weekend outings is motivation, not frustration.

To repeat, much of the envisioning process is best left up to a visionary leader. (This is especially true in working with lay volunteers, as in a church.) When given sufficient time, he will be the one to carry the vision torch. To attempt the entire envisioning process over a short time span with a group whose visionary capacities may vary from great to nonexistent is not a wise use of time. It is most important that ministry boards, especially dedicated lay boards, understand this and not attempt to rush or control the process, which, in fact, may only serve to impede the process.

Somewhere toward the end of the development stage it may be necessary to focus the vision statement. This depends on the ultimate size of the document and its purpose. More will be said about this in the next section.

The Birth of the Vision

The birth of the vision occurs at that point in time when the dream becomes the vision. Perhaps the best approach to understanding the birth of a vision is to ask and answer several important questions.

How Do You Know When You Have a Vision?

Or, at what point does the dream end and the vision begin? I believe that the answer to these questions includes a subjective as well as an objective element. Clever words and sentences on a piece of paper do not a vision make. While they are necessary from an objective standpoint, without the subjective element they tend to lie dormant on the page waiting for something to come along and wake them up or bring them to life.

The subjective element is found in the emotions and feelings the visionary experiences when the vision is born. Just as emotions and feelings accompany the birth of a child, so they should accompany the birth of a vision. But what kinds of emotions and feelings? In my personal experience I have felt a rush or flow of excitement. In that flash of time when it all comes together, there is a sense of having arrived. It feels right, clicks in such a way as to make the dreamer feel exhilarated. There is an extreme sense of ultimate accomplishment. He may walk away from the process knowing that he has reached a milestone in his ministry if not in his life.

This emotional experience is important, because it not only signals the birth of the vision but provides the motivation or impetus that leads to the ultimate realization of the vision in a ministry. We must be careful not to view the birth of the vision as an end in itself. This often happens because so much work and time have gone into its development. Now that the vision has finally arrived, there may be a temptation to sit back, relax, and thereby cut short the envisioning process.

However, a successful birth signals not the end but the beginning of the life of a vision and the ensuing ministry. Once the vision is born, it must now be communicated, implemented, and preserved if the ministry is to grow and prosper. What is it that initiates these events in the life of the ministry? I believe it can be that initial burst of enthusiasm. While the emotions connected with the birth experience tend to fade rather quickly, the memories do not. As visionary leaders cast, implement, and preserve the vision, they are reminded of the emotions surrounding its birth. The memory touches a warm place in their hearts, reminds them of how good they felt, and tends to motivate them all over again.

What Will the New Vision Look Like?

Another way to ask the same question is, How would you know a vision if you saw it? Does it have to be several pages in length? The answer depends on a number of factors. One is the contents of the statement. The more included in the document, the longer it is. The final product should be culled to a length that only includes what is necessary to understand the vision. Otherwise, it comes across as boring and risks an early death.

Another factor includes those who will read the statement, those for whom the vision was designed (the vision audience). Does the audience include a leadership team, potential donors, a unique target group, the public in general, or a combination of these? Determine the length and form of the statement that will most appeal to them. The size will expand or contract according to the amount of commitment necessary for the realization of the vision. Those who will be involved professionally in the ministry will want to know more. Those who are not will most probably require less. When in doubt, opt for brevity.

Must Anything Else Be Done to the Vision?

Most vision statements range from several paragraphs to several pages in length, but it is wise to narrow the entire statement to a slogan. In fact, what many people call a vision statement is actually a vision slogan. The result is both the larger vision document and a summary statement in the form of a slogan.

Slogans primarily help people communicate and remember the vision. They are usually very short, ranging from a few words to several sentences. After the vision audience is exposed to the broader vision document, the slogan will continually remind them of the contents of that vision document. However, a slogan may be designed so well that it communicates by itself most of the information contained within the vision document as well as reminding people of the document.

Following are the steps needed to shape the vision statement into a vision slogan, along with several examples of slogans.

First, capture the essence of the vision. The essence is what is left when all else has been stripped away. It is the very core of the vision. To alter it is to alter the whole vision. This essence then is shaped into the vision slogan.

Second, express the vision in a few words, a single sentence, or as few sentences as possible. Brevity counts, not verbosity. Short vision slogans are easily remembered; long slogan statements are easily forgotten. Any slogan that is longer than one sentence is in trouble unless it is unusually memorable. Long slogan sentences are as hard on people's memories as two or more short sentences.

Third, use creativity in structure and word choice. The repetition of similar words and numbers may work. The use of participles and infinitives can enhance structure and add necessary variety. Choose words that "grab" the listener's attention. Add an element of freshness to the slogan. In particular, opt for images and word pictures, all of which serve to render the slogan memorable.

Fourth, use language that is familiar to the vision community. It is most instructive to note how Jesus used language to communicate spiritual truth to people. For example, when he was with fishermen he spoke of fishing for men (Matt. 4:18, 19). When he was around farmers he spoke of mixing wheat with tares and sowing various soils with seed (Matt. 13:1–9, 24–30).

Finally, collect other vision statements and slogans for ideas and do not set the vision slogans in concrete. Add an element of freshness and vigor to tired slogans by periodically changing their wording or structure without changing their essence. Follow the example of McDonald's hamburger chain, which changes its slogan two or three times a year.

I have collected vision slogans both sacred and secular. Following are some church and parachurch ministry slogans which serve as good illustrations for the above steps. First, I will identify the source or author of each slogan and its ministry context. Next, I will state the slogan itself. Finally, I will offer a brief critique pointing out the unique strengths of various features found within the slogan.

Dr. Chris Marantika is the president of Indonesian Theological Seminary. A requirement for graduation from this school is that each student plant a church. The reason for this is Dr. Marantika's vision, which he has condensed into the following vision slogan:

One church, one village, one generation.

This slogan manages to capture the vision so well that one does not have to refer back to any vision statement to understand it. The essence of this slogan is Marantika's strategy to sow the Great Commission across the soil of Indonesia. However, the terms *Great Commission* or *Commission* are not explicitly stated but understood from the context of the seminary and its ministry. This is preferable over use of the actual terms, for the sake of brevity and variety.

The slogan itself consists of only six words, three of which are the same word *one*. This makes it all but impossible to forget. In fact, I heard this slogan only once and have never forgotten it. The mind through either the eye or the ear has little trouble spotting and focusing on the slogan because of its repetition and overall brevity.

The structure of the slogan is exemplary. The repetition and placement of the word *one* is attractive to the mind because it says this slogan will be easy to comprehend and remember.

The slogan primarily communicates the ministry's strategy, structured as a progression through the clever placement of the words *church, village,* and *generation.* The word *church* identifies what Dr. Marantika wants to accomplish: to plant churches through his students. The word *village* tells where these churches will be located. His vision is that the seminary will "salt" every village in Indonesia with churches. Finally, the word *generation* tells when. He hopes to accomplish this dream in his generation.

I would be surprised if Dr. Marantika went through this kind of analysis to generate his vision. Most likely, it flashed unexpectedly into his mind one morning while he drove to work. The same is probably true of the following slogans as well.

My friend Brad Smith and Bob Hendricks have a desire to plant a church in the city of Washington, D.C. Due to illness their vision has not yet been realized. They have developed a vision statement and condensed it into the following slogan:

Building a community to reach a community.
Reaching a community to change a city.
Changing a city to reach a nation.

Several noteworthy features are found in this slogan. As does Dr. Marantika's slogan, this one also communicates the essence of the vision, the Great Commission, by using the word *reach.*

This vision slogan illustrates well creative word choice and structure. *Community* is repeated three times, the first to refer to the core group or ministry community, the other two to the target community.

Each sentence begins with a participle followed by an infinitive that expresses purpose. Building the ministry community is for the purpose of reaching or evangelizing the target community, which ultimately will include the other communities in the city and will therefore change the City of Washington. Because of the influence the city has on the rest of this country, changing the city aids the evangelizing of the entire nation.

Dr. Marantika's slogan includes a progression explaining the what, where, and when of his vision, whereas this one includes both the goal and the strategy for accomplishing that goal.

I wear several "hats" in my work at Dallas Seminary. One is in preparing students and graduates of the seminary to be church planters. As stated previously, I believe that, in light of the present decline in the American church, God will seed this country with a significant number of new churches over the next several decades. It is a part of my vision that Dallas Seminary supply its share of pastors to start these churches. Consequently, I have developed the following vision statement:

My vision is to evangelize and disciple the nonchurched in America and abroad by recruiting and equipping 200 Dallas Seminary students and alumni to plant a minimum of 200 dynamic, growing churches by the year 2000.

I have further reduced this vision statement to the following vision slogan:

200 by 2000

This slogan has several features worth noting. Its strongest feature is its brevity. It is a numerical slogan consisting of two numbers that are very different in their amounts but are very similar in both sound and appearance. This makes it visually catching and "sticky" (memorable).

The slogan accomplishes several purposes. First, although it calls attention to the vision, unlike the two slogans above, it alone does not communicate the whole vision. A person would need prior knowledge of the vision statement; then the slogan would be a reminder of the contents of that vision statement. Actually, this is how the slogan is intended to function. The other two above slogans are unusual in that they not only call attention to the dream but also communicate the dream itself.

Second, my slogan intentionally focuses on certain aspects of the vision. The number 200 identifies both who and how many and calls attention to the numerical goals of the vision, which are 200 church planters and 200 churches. The number 2000 identifies when and signals the time or deadline for accomplishing the vision, which is the year 2000. The reason for this focus is the environment in which I primarily use the slogan, which is a seminary campus. To add to the effect of this slogan, I usually attach it to my church-planting logo, which I will say more about in the section on communicating the vision.

In 1980, Pastor Rick Warren planted Saddleback Valley Community Church in Mission Viejo, California. Since that time the church has grown from seven people to over 4000 in attendance. What is so exciting about this growth is that much of it is conversion rather than transfer growth. Pastor Warren has condensed his vision statement into the following slogan:

A great commitment to the great commandment and the Great Commission will create a great church.

Of the important features of this slogan the first is that it is brief and limited to only one sentence. Second is the repetition of at least five words that begin with the letter *c:* commitment, commandment, commission, create, and church. This serves to catch attention and help the slogan stick.

Third is the repetition of the word *great* throughout the slogan, which sends a clear message that Saddleback is not interested in simply being just another church but has high aspirations. It does not want to be known as an average church; it plans to reach its full potential and be a great church. This is because it has both a great commandment and a Great Commission.

The essence of the slogan is commitment. This is a strong term communicating that Saddleback is very serious about its vision and its mission. This commitment is based on two critical elements. The first is the "great commandment" in Matthew 22:36–40, Christ's commandment to love God with all your heart and your neighbor as yourself. The second element is the Great Commission to evangelize and edify. The key to becoming a great church in God's eyes is the strongest of commitments to love him and pursue his Great Commission.

Following are several other vision slogans from my collection. The Center for Christian Leadership at Dallas Seminary in Dallas, Texas: "Building leaders to disciple the nations." Wayne McDonald, who is planting Metrocrest Community Church in Coppell, Texas: "Reaching up . . . reaching out." Mike Baer, who leads a group in Atlanta, Georgia: "Bringing Christ to men and men to Christ." Union Gospel Mission, a Christian ministry to the homeless and street people in Dallas, Texas: "Helping the last, the least, the lost." Finally, Fellowship Bible Church of Park Cities in Dallas, Texas: "Meeting the needs of contemporary people through Christ."

Secular organizations have vision slogans that can be helpful examples. One of the telephone companies encourages us to "Reach out and touch someone." A florist in the Dallas metroplex has this on its delivery trucks: "We don't sell flowers, we sell beauty." A bank advertises: "Innovative banking for innovative companies."

The development of the vision statement is complete when it has been condensed to the vision slogan. However, the envisioning process is by no means complete. It would be a grave error if the ministry relaxed at this point. Actually, much lies ahead, as will be seen in the next chapter.

It's a Vision!

Communicating the Vision

"I'm going to bed, dear, are you coming soon?" asked Mary.

Pastor Bob replied, "Yeah, I'll be there in a minute."

"Sure you will!" Mary mumbled as she shook her head and slid under the covers. She awoke about an hour later, according to the clock by her bed, because of several strong contractions. Sure enough, Bob was still up.

He had tried to break away from the book, but he was so excited that he knew he could not possibly sleep. Why bother? There were too many stimulating ideas dancing inside his head. As he read about the process of birthing the vision, a dream began to take shape in his mind. It seemed to come from out of nowhere. As he read more about the process, he began to walk his dream through that process, and the result was exciting. It was not yet a vision, but it was a creative start. He chuckled to himself. Mary was on the verge of birthing another baby. Could it be that he was about to birth a vision as well? But what was next? Obviously the book contained several more chapters. What else needed to be said? He was curious, so he looked at the next chapter. The title concerned the communication of the vision. This made perfect sense. You do not just birth a vision and then keep it quiet.

His thoughts were interrupted by a call from the bedroom. Mary was having strong contractions. She was not due for another two weeks, but their son had been born earlier than expected. Over the next hour the contractions intensified and came closer together. She knew it was time to go to the hospital.

Hours later Pastor Bob burst from the sterile delivery room wearing a white gown around his body, a big grin on his face, and "It's a boy!" on his lips. Rushing over to anxious grandparents and joyous friends, he repeated the news over and over amid backslaps and pumping handshakes. But the communication of the joyous event did not stop there. After all the hugs and handshakes, the exuberant father with a roll of quarters in his pocket moved to a nearby phone for a round of calls.

Why all the commotion? The birth of a child is a joyous, momentous occasion. It is a time to celebrate and communicate the joy of new life and what God has done. How could anyone not declare such a wonderful event?

The birth of a child parallels in many ways the birth of a vision. Both are exciting, momentous occasions that demand communication of their existence to all those in the natural family or the ministry community. To birth a vision without conveying the vision would be as strange as birthing a child and not sending out birth announcements. Yet, this happens in some well-meaning ministries. They develop and birth the vision but miss the importance of passing on the vision, thus frustrating themselves and risking a premature burial of the entire process. The purpose of this chapter is to explain the process for announcing the birth of the vision and to offer some practical methods for communicating the vision to the ministry community and the ministry constituency.

The Vision Casting Process

Communicating the news of a profound, significant vision for the future of a ministry involves a sender, a message, and a receiver. These are basic to any communication process and vital to the ultimate realization of any goal or vision. It is important for the leadership of a ministry organization to think through these three areas of conveying their unique vision before they actually begin the process.

The Conveyers

The first step before announcing any vision is to determine who will take the responsibility for casting and conveying the vision. This should be the responsibility of everyone who is a part of the ministry: the primary leader, other leaders, and followers.

PRIMARY LEADER. As was said in chapter 3, conveying the vision becomes the primary responsibility of the visionary leader who is the organization's point person and, by virtue of the position, most likely its primary spokesperson. In the parachurch organization this person is often the president or founder of the ministry. In the church this individual will in most cases be the pastor in the smaller church and the senior pastor in the larger church.

I have suggested earlier that one of the primary functions of the visionary leader of any ministry is that of vision caster. This is practically assumed in most parachurch ministries; it is the leader's responsibility to travel, represent the ministry, and thus spread the vision as well as to raise the necessary finances to fund the ministry.

However, this has not been the case in most churches. The role of the pastor usually includes such responsibilities as teacher, preacher, evangelist, and chaplain. While most churches desire a biblical role for their pastor, the position has been affected as much by their culture as by Scripture. This can be seen in the wide variety of pastoral functions in various rural and urban settings across America. I believe that the Scriptures purposefully provide certain broad responsibilities for pastors rather than precise details, which allows them freedom and flexibility within the various cultural settings in which they minister both in America and around the world.

In light of the importance of vision to the local church, I propose a new paradigm for the pastoral role, which I believe will help to accomplish the Great Commission in the twenty-first century. This includes such key pastoral functions as being the primary communicator, the developer of present and potential leadership, and the primary caster of the vision.

It is this latter responsibility that concerns us here. I divide the vision casting process into three parts. The first is that of vision cultivator. Here the pastor takes the responsibility of initiating and developing the ministry's vision. The second is vision communicator. This involves the process of regularly holding up the vision before the ministry community. The third is vision clarifier. The primary function here is to focus the vision by regularly rethinking it and seeking to further refine it and apply it within and outside the confines of the ministry.

While it is the primary responsibility of the point person in a ministry to communicate the vision, that person cannot do it alone. Thus, it becomes imperative that he ignite others with the same vision so that they, in turn, achieve ownership and become vision casters as well.

OTHER LEADERS. Who are these other people? Initially they will comprise the other primary and secondary leaders on the team, whether they are hired as in some parachurch situations or voluntary such as the elder board of a church. In chapter 3 I called them significant others. Their role is to follow the visionary's leadership, to aid in developing the dream, to rally support behind it, and to pass it on to as many people as possible.

Most ministries have other leaders as well but at a secondary or lower level. They must not be overlooked in the casting process. Often they work with people at the grassroots level and wield enough influence to either accelerate or impede the progress of the vision. This assumes that the leader meets regularly with and feeds into the lives of these people as well as of those at the other levels. This is a must in any ministry, especially in churches where the majority of these faithful people are volunteers. Far too often they are asked to take some responsibility and then are abandoned to fend for themselves. The result is a high dropout rate. The role of the leader in this case is to keep the vision before them, encourage them in their walk with the Savior, and make sure they have the skills necessary to accomplish well their individual ministries.

FOLLOWERS. Finally, it is important that those who are the followers in the ministry be vision casters. These people are the employees or volunteer workers in the parachurch and the members and regular attenders in the church. They are not only the people at the grass-roots level, they are the grass roots. They make up the audience of the visionary and are the ones who need to be convinced of the vision, for ultimately they are the people who are to be led in accomplishing the vision. The goal is that they not only catch the vision, but that they, in turn, cast the vision.

A point person in a ministry who casts a vision for that ministry will accomplish far more for Christ's kingdom than one who has no vision. However, recruiting those in leadership and those at the ministry's grass-roots level as a coalition of vision casters, places the efforts of the entire ministry community behind the efforts of the point person. In fact, this is the very strategy the Savior used in promoting the Great Commission vision among his apostles and those disciples who were a part of the early church in Acts and beyond. Indeed, this kind of force is unstoppable and practically guarantees tremendous progress toward the realization of the dream.

The Message

The next step which is basic to any communication process is the determination of the message. The leader must have a message. Of course, that message for the visionary leader is the vision. This may all seem rather elementary, yet too many people in positions of leadership around the world either do not have a vision or they do not have a clear vision, or they do not see the need to articulate that vision.

In general, the contents of the vision for Christian ministry have already been discussed in chapter 4. There it was determined that the essential vision for the church was established in the first century A.D. by Christ as the Great Commission. The vision for parachurch ministries is either the Commission or is subsumed under it. For example, the vision for an organization might be the evangelization of children or college students on the secular campus. The vision of another could be the writing and publication of literature that promotes discipleship and Christian maturity.

The purpose of this section is not to reiterate again the contents of the vision but to present two other key factors that affect the communication of the vision message.

COMPREHENSION. The first factor in effective communication is the comprehension of the vision. The question is, Do people understand the dream? The visionary leader can capitalize on every conceivable opportunity to convey the vision, but if no one understands the vision, then as far as the ministry is concerned there is no vision. Since we have already addressed the development and wording of the vision statement, the purpose here is to focus on the kind of context in which to most effectively present the vision for clearest comprehension of it.

Certainly, a concise, well-worded vision statement and slogan greatly affect the clarity of the vision. Often they alone may sufficiently convey the dream. But other factors will help to clarify the vision as well. One is the necessity of presenting the vision within the context of a critical deficiency or problem with the status quo. Most commonly, this is the main thing that inspired the visionary to cultivate the vision in the first place. This being the case, it would seem that communicating the vision could follow the same process: the vision becomes the solution to that deficiency or problem.

This need or deficiency is first described in a speech or sermon to be followed by the vision-solution.

A classic example is the presentation of the gospel as God's vision for all mankind. Most presentations begin not with the gospel but man's need for the gospel. In Romans 3:23, Paul exposes the sinful state of mankind when he writes, "For all have sinned and come short of the glory of God." Next, in Romans 6:23, he warns that this sin will culminate some day in spiritual death: "For the wages of sin is death, but the free gift of God is eternal life in Christ Jesus our Lord." Finally, to those who believe that their good works merit eternal favor with God, Paul writes in Ephesians 2:8, 9, "For by grace you have been saved through faith; and that not of yourselves, it is the gift of God; not as a result of works, that no one should boast." Now that the spiritual problem has been communicated, listeners often sense their dire need and are ready to hear the gospel or the good news, which is the only solution to that problem.

A second classic example is God communicating his vision for his people during Nehemiah's life. In the historical context of Jerusalem's ruined walls and gates and distressed people God raised up Nehemiah as his visionary to lead the people out of their desperate situation. In Nehemiah's first message to the people he began by reminding them of their desperate problem, which he called their reproach. Then he invited them to join him in rebuilding the wall, which not only symbolized the vision but was the solution to their problem (Neh. 2:17, 18).

Another context in which to present the vision is that of an untapped, unexploited spiritual opportunity. Sometimes this also figures in the initial development of the vision. Thus, it, too, would serve well in conveying the vision to a ministry community. In a speech or sermon the vision is presented in the context of the opportunity that motivates and catalyzes people to action. A good example is the recent spiritual awakening that broke out in 1989 in Mombasa, Kenya. God in his sovereignty decided to reach down and bring a considerable number of people of this region to himself. Thus, a revival of immense proportion is taking place, and large numbers of people are coming to faith in Christ. Good missions strategy says that as many people as possible should be quickly recruited and sent to this area to help bring in the spiritual harvest.

In recruiting workers to go to Mombasa, mission representatives could present the Great Commission vision in the context of this great East African revival. This context proves most attractive for several reasons. The revival is current and the situation calls for reaping the harvest, not the arduous process of sowing. Second, there is a sense of urgency. Most revivals last only a short period of time; thus people need to go now before it is too late. Third, this requires a short-term, not a long-term personal commitment. No one need become a career missionary in Africa. Consequently, presenting the Great Commission vision in this context of great opportunity would and has inspired many to join forces with those in the region to win the people for Christ.

CREDIBILITY. A second key factor which affects the communication of the vision-message is the credibility of the vision. The first factor asks, Do they understand it? The second asks, Do they believe in it? Any mission vision must have credibility if people are to believe in and commit themselves to it. Three elements can contribute to a credible, acceptable vision-message.

The visionary leader's performance. People want to know the "track record" of the visionary leader. This consists of such features as God's evident blessing on a person's life and ministry, prior ministry success, strong gifts and abilities, strong communication skills, personal dedication to the cause, and a commitment to biblical values. Does the leader show extraordinary ability in any or most of these features?

When it becomes evident that God is uniquely blessing leaders' lives and ministries, they gain extraordinary credibility in the eyes of their followers and even the general public. Sometimes God grants special favor in a person's ministry in such a way that former obstacles are removed and doors which normally are closed are opened.

An excellent example is in Nehemiah's vision speech where he explains, "And I told them how the hand of my God had been favorable to me, and also about the king's words which he had spoken to me" (Neh. 2:18). This is a reference to verse 14 where the pagan king, Artaxerxes, agrees to write a letter permitting Nehemiah to return to Judah and another letter to certain individuals to supply him with the necessary resources to rebuild the gates and wall of Jerusalem.

There is no indication in the text that Nehemiah's audience knew him well. Thus, it is not surprising that he tells them of God's special hand on his work so that he might gain some credibility. This must have worked, because God granted him favor again, and the people responded to his challenge and agreed to pursue the vision.

Prior ministry experience communicates credibility in Christian circles. I have observed that usually it is the fact of the experience alone and not necessarily the quality of the experience that brings credibility, especially in the selection of pastors for churches. And highly successful prior ministry experience communicates high credibility, and even a following in some cases.

The presence of strong gifts or abilities also conveys credibility, especially in the area of Christian leadership. There is a great need today for men and women with leadership expertise who can direct ministries with sustained excellence. This is because a vacuum created by the retirement of many older leaders has not yet been filled by a younger generation of leadership. Consequently, if a person has demonstrated strong leadership gifts and abilities, he or she is given high marks on the report card of credibility.

Another area that rates high is expertise as a pulpiteer, especially as the ministry increases in size. People are generally impressed by a good communicator, that is, an "up front" ministry which has exposure to more people than other ministries such as counseling. This, coupled with the fact that currently there are not a large number of leaders known for their abilities in the pulpit, results in strong credibility.

Finally, the personal dedication of the leader to the cause creates trustworthiness for the vision. If leaders expect their followers to commit themselves to the cause, then those leaders must demonstrate their own high commitment to the cause. Leaders accomplish this through strong personal dedication to the dream that manifests itself in self-sacrifice and personal risk taking. Generally, the perception is: the greater the self-sacrifice or personal risk, the greater the trustworthiness of the cause.

The content of the vision. Another element that affects people's acceptance of the vision-message is the content of the vision itself. Does it convince them of its own value? At issue is whether or not the vision is based on Scripture. When visionaries are able to point to a particular biblical reference in support of their dream, they catch the attention of those in the Christian community who have a high view of Scripture. Most churches and parachurch organizations are able to do this because the church's vision is the Great Commission and most parachurch visions are subsumed under that Commission.

Content credibility also depends on the relationship between the vision and the ministry community's felt needs. People award high credibility to dreams that address and offer solutions to their felt needs. Again, the Jews in Nehemiah's day were in "great distress" (Neh. 1:3) and were considered a "reproach" (Neh. 2:17b). Nehemiah's vision to "rebuild the wall of Jerusalem" (Neh. 2:17a) was a clear, long-awaited solution to the kind of felt needs they lived with and thought about on a daily basis.

Finally is the relationship between the dream and some untapped opportunity. A vision that is highly sensitive to some obvious spiritual opportunity elicits believability. An example is the current focus by some individuals and churches on reaching America's nonchurched people. The number of churches in America is declining while the number of nonchurched Americans is increasing. A survey by George Gallup reveals this and also the fact that these nonchurched people are very interested in spiritual things.[1] Some visionaries have brought together the church's decline with the growth of the nonchurched and their spiritual interest to demonstrate a great opportunity to plant churches that will target and reach vast numbers of nonchurched Americans.

The visionary leader's integrity. A third element that affects the people's acceptance of the vision-message is the vision caster's character. Leaders who display integrity and trustworthiness are given high credibility by those within and outside the ministry community. Actually, the Christian community in general and the church in particular are directed to assign credibility on the basis of character. This is clearly spelled out in various passages such as 1 Timothy 3:1–13 and Titus 1:5–9, which detail the character qualifications for Christian leadership in the church.

Character is the foundation of Christian leadership. A person's entire ministry and leadership rest on his or her character. If the character is flawed in some way, then the ministry will be flawed proportionately. This has been demonstrated in the late 1980s by the fall of a number of popular television evangelists. However, in my position at a theological seminary, I observed that this time was also characterized by the fall of an unusually high number of pastors and some parachurch leaders as well. Indeed, the late 1980s were difficult days for those in professional ministry positions. As might be expected, the reaction from both the Christian community and the secular community was to question the credibility of Christian organizations in general. For many, the number-one question concerning the leadership of any Christian organization involved the integrity of that leadership.

The Receiver

The third step in conveying the vision is to consider those who will receive it. They are the ministry audience whom I divide into two groups: the ministry community and the ministry constituency. Actually the purpose for communicating the vision is that the ministry audience own the dream and become the vision audience. When this takes place, the ministry community and the constituency become the vision community and constituency. Both the terms *ministry community* and *ministry constituency* need further clarification.

The ministry community consists of all those who are directly involved in implementing the ministry vision. In a parachurch ministry they are the people who make up the ministry from the president or point person to the part-time volunteer helper. For example, in a Christian school it would include the administration, faculty, staff, student body, and parent/community supporters/helpers. In the church it includes the pastoral staff, various boards, secretarial and custodial help, and the members and regular attenders.

It is critical to the success of any ministry that these people both comprehend and own the vision. The idea is that all the people own the vision, from the president to the mail clerk or from the pastor to the custodian. The principle is simple. The more people involved in the accomplishment of the vision, the greater the likelihood of its realization. Good dream casting wins recruits who enlarge the ministry team behind the vision. When this takes place, the ministry community becomes the empowered vision community.

The ministry constituency consists of those who are outside the ministry community. They may relate to a parachurch ministry by praying regularly for it or by contributing financially to it. They may also be recipients of the ministry in the sense that they benefit from it in some way such as do a radio audience or those on a mailing list. They may relate to a church ministry by occasional attendance, prayer, or even financial support. In either case, it is not essential that these people understand the vision and normally most do not. However, a wise ministry team will do everything possible to communicate the vision to the ministry constituency so that they may become as much as possible an empowered visionary constituency. This, too, serves to increase even more the size of the army and its potential for accomplishing the dream.

In the above discussion, the vision audience is described as an empowered vision community and an empowered vision constituency. What does the term *empowered* mean? I do not use this term here from a strict biblical or theological perspective, as when a Christian is empowered by the Holy Spirit for ministry (Eph. 3:20), although this should be true of the people in each community. Instead, I use the term more from a leadership perspective.

In leadership, empowerment involves giving people within the organization the necessary authority and power to take responsibility for the success of their individual parts of the ministry so that the organization strongly moves toward the achievement of its vision. Thus, empowerment applies more to those in the ministry community than those in the ministry constituency but could include the latter.

Empowerment primarily affects the accomplishment of the vision once it is communicated. However, it affects the communication of the vision in that empowered people not only move to implement the vision, but they are good vision casters as well. Because they are sold on the vision and have strongly committed themselves to it, they become infectious in spreading the dream to other people with whom they come in contact.

Practical Methods for Casting the Vision

The purpose of the rest of this chapter is not to elaborate all the fine points of the communication of a concept. This can be done more effectively by consulting a text on speech communication or homiletics. Instead, this portion will feature a variety of practical methods to facilitate the casting of the ministry vision. It should be kept in mind throughout these pages that a key to articulating the vision is to be constantly communicating the vision using as many of these methods as possible. The problem is that most people have short memories. Visions are no exception. Most vision casters agree that it takes about one month for people to forget the vision. Consequently, a vision for the future is not a once-for-all kind of thing. The ministry must have a number of different methods for regularly "parading" its dream by its people. And several of these methods should take place at the same time. In short, the rule is, Repeat it over and over every day in a different way.

The Visionary's Life

The leader's life communicates the vision by modeling the message. A basic requirement for a dream caster is that he first owns the vision. Ownership here implies a genuine, personal commitment to the vision. This is evident when the vision excites and motivates him to the point that he finds himself constantly thinking, dreaming, and talking about it. There will be times when those closest to him will be tempted to accuse him of having a one-track mind. In some cases, the dream will keep him awake at night. In other words, the leader personifies the dream. He has a profound sense that he can make a difference and that the world will be a better place because of his dream. He is so convinced of his vision that not to act would seem to him a grave injustice.

An example of this kind of personal commitment to a vision is the apostle Paul. Early in his ministry his vision was to reach his people, the Jews, for Christ. He expresses the vision in Romans 10:1, where he says, "Brethren, my heart's desire and my prayer to God for them is for their salvation." His intense, personal commitment to this mission is expressed in Romans 9:3, where he states that he is willing to go so far as to be accursed, eternally separated from Christ, if it would mean the eternal salvation of his people according to the flesh.

For the leader to personify the vision accomplishes several things. First he models visionary behavior for the ministry team. They watch him to see how a dream affects a person's life. His behavior answers their question, How will our dreaming the same dream affect our lives? This tends to set a new spirit among the people. They know what they can expect from him and the kind of behavior he expects from them.

Next, the leader's life brings credibility to the vision and the ministry. People, especially followers, constantly observe the leader's life for evidence of credibility. Many ask on a conscious as well as a subconscious level, "Is this person qualified to lead us? Why should I follow him or her?" In particular, they look to outward behavior as a chief indicator of credibility. The very thing that communicates credibility is the visionary leader's passion for the vision. When people see the emotional impact the vision has on the leader's life, they grant that leader considerable credibility. In the same manner, should the leader become disillusioned or discouraged and is no longer inflamed by the vision, that leader will lose credibility with his or her constituency. A leader who has lost the vision and who tries to lead people is trying to light a fire with a wet match.

Finally, when leaders personify the vision they motivate others to support and own the vision for themselves. A leader's enthusiasm is infectious, and others catch the vision. They believe that if the vision excites and motivates someone in the leader's position, it must be valuable and worth following. Their response, in turn, motivates still others and spreads enthusiasm throughout the entire ministry community moving them closer to becoming a vision community.

In a discussion of the role of vision in successful churches, George Barna summarizes the impact of personifying the vision in the following:

> In successful churches, people were encouraged to articulate the vision through lifestyle, not just the repetition of the right words. While the degree of emphasis placed upon this type of commitment varied from church to church, all of the growing churches clearly believed that behavioral modeling was the most effective means of communicating a concept to people. Thus, a vision that did not translate into overt action by the people was a vision that had little real support and ownership.

Lacking such support and ownership, the vision—and, probably, the church—would fail to grow.[2]

The Visionary's Message

Second, the leader's message communicates the vision. In the parachurch ministry, the message most often takes the form of a sermon or a speech usually delivered to a gathering of the entire ministry team. In the church, the message most often takes the form of a sermon which is delivered typically on Sunday morning to the membership. The sermon or speech is a primary vehicle of the vision caster, and it is these speaking occasions which provide the visionary with an ideal opportunity to cast the vision. However, a real danger for the church in particular is when the sermon or speech is viewed as the only vehicle for communicating the vision. Several important elements facilitate communicating the vision through a sermon or speech.

UNDERSTAND THE AUDIENCE. The first is to speak with understanding. The speaker must know and understand the audience, which most likely is the people who make up the ministry community. This means the leader has spent enough time with the people to genuinely accept and understand them. To do less results in great difficulty in understanding and leading those people.

The ministry community must know and believe that the leader understands their needs, dreams, hopes, and aspirations. People know that a leader cannot find solutions to their needs or turn their dreams into reality until that leader knows and understands those needs and dreams. Indeed, most often visions are cast in the form of solutions to people's needs. If based on a wrong understanding of people's needs and hurts, solutions will come across as irrelevant and insipid.

The ministry community also needs to understand how the vision affects or benefits them. The leader who knows and understands their needs and hopes can communicate this knowledge to them in his messages through practical illustrations and stories from their lives and his own. Next, and key to their comprehension of the vision, he must demonstrate how the vision is the solution to their problems or the realization of their hopes. For example, a message can show how too many churches in America fall far short of reaching their communities with the gospel, and can demonstrate a need for increasing evangelistic efforts toward those communities. However, it is critical to show that winning the community to Christ means winning the members' friends, next door neighbors, and possibly families for the Savior as well.

USE EXPRESSIVE LANGUAGE. A second element which facilitates communicating the vision through a speech or sermon is the use of expressive language, a powerful tool in the hands of visionary leaders. Expressive language enables people to hear, feel, sense, and see the dream. The goal is to turn abstract terms into concrete terms and to make the intangible tangible. This is accomplished through the use of certain language vehicles such as stories, figures of speech, and carefully worded slogans.

Storytelling is a universal means of conveying information. The method is found in most cultures and has been around since the creation of man. Everybody loves a good story. Consequently, it is a very effective tool that is a "must" for the visionary communicator.

We can observe the effective use of storytelling in both the Old Testament and the New. For example, in 1 Samuel 12 Nathan the prophet told King David the story of how a rich man abused a poor man by taking his only lamb and using it for his personal ends. Nathan used this story to help King David realize and come to grips with the extent of his sin. The Gospels as narrative literature repeatedly communicate divine truth through telling the story of the life of Christ and his disciples. The Book of Acts tells the story of what happened after the ascension of Christ, and how God used the disciples in birthing and growing the early church.

Leaders who desire to communicate the dream must do so with stories. Indeed, Conger in *The Charismatic Leader* writes that in communicating a vision in a business setting, stories encourage more commitment than other means such as statistics.[3] One very effective way to accomplish this in ministry is for the leader to tell his own story, his personal testimony of the impact the vision has had on his life. If the vision involves evangelism, he might tell the story of how he came to faith in Christ. The apostle Paul did this when he gave his testimony to a crowd of Jews (Acts 22) and before Agrippa (Acts 26). He addressed mostly unbelievers, and the Holy Spirit recorded this account of Paul's vision to convey it to us twentieth-century readers.

The speaker can also tell the success stories of others. For example, there are probably other ministries similar to his which have been amazingly blessed of God. Possibly one has influenced him and his vision as mentor or model. The history of these ministries and experiences of their leaders can be obtained from someone in or near the ministry, on tapes, or in articles or books that recount stories about the ministry and its leader. Stories of their visions and experiences can help convey others' visions.

Another effective means is to tell the stories of others who have come to Christ through the implementation of the vision. In demonstrating the effectiveness of friendship evangelism as a tool for accomplishing the Great Commission vision, I often tell the story of how one young housewife in our congregation developed a friendship with an unchurched neighbor who was about the same age. The neighbor was also a housewife who happened to be experiencing difficulty in her marriage. The Christian wife did a lot of patient listening and loaned her neighbor a book or two on marriage from a Christian perspective. It was only a matter of time before the neighbor accepted Christ.

Vision conveyers should liberally sprinkle their vision messages with figures of speech. Metaphors and similes can be highly effective. For example, earlier in this chapter I used the metaphor of trying to light a fire with a wet match.

Earlier in this book I stressed the importance of giving a vision adequate time to develop by comparing that process to baking a potato: "The dream must be carefully wrapped in the foil of creativity and baked slowly, very slowly, in the oven of time."

Figures of speech add vividness and tangibility to what otherwise could be an intangible dream. No doubt some speakers use them more easily than do others. Some people naturally think visually. They are working on a concept, and a metaphor or a simile pops inherently into their minds. Those who find that this does not come naturally should try to train themselves to think visually by reviewing their messages or sermons and attempting to visualize their contents, translating key concepts into mental pictures, recording and verbalizing them.

Not only can the dream itself be communicated through a slogan, but critical concepts which are a part of the dream can often be summed up and communicated through a well-worded slogan. The use of slogans in communicating a vision was discussed in the previous chapter. Here I would like to elaborate on the use of the slogan to express various concepts that are subsumed under the dream. For example, the vision for Christ's church has already been determined by him as the Great Commission. However, numerous concepts that can relate directly to the Commission are subsumed under it.

One is the importance of each believer's commitment to use his or her spiritual gifts to edify the entire church body as explained in 1 Corinthians 12–14. This affects lay mobilization and the ministry of all the parts of Christ's body in the accomplishment of the church's mission. A popular slogan that captures this concept is, "Every member a minister." Its effect lies in the fact that it is succinct, alliterates *member* and *minister*, and contains the inclusive word *every*. Also, the use of the word *minister* for laypeople communicates the desired depth of personal commitment.

I have sensed among Christians of the baby boom generation a lack of commitment to the church that is vital to the

Great Commission. Therefore, I have developed a slogan to emphasize the need for intense commitment on the part of lay Christian boomers. I encourage them to be "completely committed Christians." The constant exhortation in moving any ministry community toward the realization of the dream is that we be "completely committed Christians." The slogan attempts to create an effect by repeating three words that begin with the same letter. Extra emphasis is placed on the word *committed* by placing the word *completely* in juxtaposition to it.

Parachurch ministries can benefit by developing articulate slogans as well. For example, in my ministry with students at Dallas Seminary I speak of "preparing a new generation to lead with sustained excellence." Again, my vision slogan at the seminary is "200 by 2000." If this slogan is effective, then it should serve to remind people that my vision is to "evangelize and disciple the nonchurched in America and abroad by recruiting and equipping 200 Dallas Seminary students and alumni to plant a minimum of 200 dynamic growing churches by the year 2000." The accomplishment of this vision is based squarely on the leadership abilities of Dallas graduates, many of whom are baby boomers. The older graduates are reaching retirement age, creating a growing need to replace them with a new generation of leadership. But these recent graduates must be leaders as well as Bible teachers. If we are to make an effective assault on the secular strongholds of this age, then it is imperative that seminaries train men and women whose leadership is characterized by excellence, that is, a reputation for sustained excellence. Church and parachurch ministries are not only looking for graduates who know the Scriptures, they are looking for leaders who know the Scriptures. The cry today is for excellence in leadership as well as in scholarship.

SPEAK POSITIVELY. A third element which facilitates the articulation of the dream through a speech or sermon is speaking positively, not negatively. An emphasis on negatives over the years has characterized the church more than the parachurch. Sometimes well-intentioned preachers com-municate a "gloom and doom" message Sunday after Sunday. The result is a "gloom and doom" attitude on the part of the sermon audience, which has proved generally ineffective when compared with a more positive style.

There are several reasons why positive preaching inspires a profound vision. First, positive preaching is sustaining, whereas negative preaching is draining. There is energy in visionary preachers. They are dynamic people who commu-nicate with vigor and life. The result is that God uses their messages to inspire and invigorate their followers. People hear them and realize they can accomplish what God expects because he is the power in their lives. Ultimately, they are energized to achieve their God-given potential in light of their unique divine design. Negative preaching has the opposite effect. It has a way of draining energy from its hearers. People come away convinced they cannot and probably will not ever accomplish anything of significance for God. They are sinners and, therefore, insignificant people with little worth.

Second, positive preaching is encouraging, whereas nega-tive preaching is discouraging. Here visionary preachers assume the role of cheerleader. Their goal is to rally people behind the dream, to enlist them for the cause of the Savior. They persuade people to look at what they can do, not what they cannot do. Positive sermons have an uplifting effect. They infuse hope and inspire followers to attempt their very best. Positive sermons acknowledge each believer's personal worth and significance that they have in Christ. They also convey optimism about life in general from the perspective of Romans 8:28 which says that "God causes all things to work together for good to those who love God, to those who are called according to His purpose." Constant negative preaching can take the heart out of people. After a while, they are brought down to a point where they question their own significance and the value of any service on their part for God.

By encouraging positive preaching, I do not propose never speaking out against a particular issue or ignoring sin in the lives of the people. Rather, I encourage avoiding the kind of negative preaching that seeks to motivate through false guilt, patronization, and manipulation. Avoid causing situations where people leave the service every week having been tongue lashed or "Bible whipped" and being aware of their sins and shortcomings but with no understanding of God's grace and the love and forgiveness of Christ. These instruments found in the toolboxes of most negative preachers who employ them week after week ultimately serve not to edify but to demean people and the cause of Christ.

CHARISMA. A fourth element which aids the communication of the vision through a sermon or speech is charisma. I almost hesitate to use this term, because it has been so overused and misunderstood in both the world of leadership and theology. I do not use the term in the sense it is used today in the more experience-oriented churches, particularly those churches that strongly emphasize the presence of all the gifts of the Spirit for this day and time and the need to manifest them in the public services of the church as well as in the privacy of members' homes. Often these churches are said to be charismatic and their pastors are described as charismatic. Neither do I use the term *charisma* as if it were some mystical or mysterious experience or that it describes the effect some leaders have on people because of some mystical, exotic personality trait.

I use the term here to describe the speaker's delivery. How a speaker delivers a message may communicate as much or more than what the speaker says in the message, whether it be nonverbal or verbal. In the field of public speaking in general and homiletics in particular, charisma has to do with voice inflection, gestures, facial expressions, and eye contact. People described as charismatic are more animated in these behaviors than people not described as charismatic.

In commenting on leadership charisma, Kouzes and Posner sum up the study of social scientists who have investigated charisma as observable behavior. They discovered that in general those perceived as charismatic were characterized by the following:

> They smiled more, spoke faster, pronounced words more clearly, and moved their heads and bodies more often. They were also likely to touch others during greetings. What we call charisma can better be understood as human expressiveness.[4]

Charismatic speakers have strong personal convictions reflected in such traits as self-confidence, expertise in their fields, extreme dedication to the cause, and a genuine concern for the needs of other people, which they charismatically express through their behavior, personal appearance, body language, and clothing. The result is that their messages have spark and ignite their followers.

For several years I taught a beginning homiletics course at Dallas Theological Seminary. While some of the men in the course had prior preaching experience, the majority were novices in the pulpit. Most, in time, developed the skills necessary to construct a biblical, reasonably well-developed sermon. A primary difference between those students who were effective communicators and those who were not was charisma. Those who were animated and expressive spoke with passion and moved and influenced the rest of us even in a sterile classroom environment. Those who had not yet developed charisma found that their sermons, though carefully exegeted and constructed, fell on deaf ears. They appeared as somewhat plastic, and their sermons had no punch. They left their listeners unmotivated and unmoved by the challenge of the sermon.

I believe that certain temperaments naturally display more charisma than others. However, those temperaments that display less charisma can develop some proficiency in its use in communication. Consequently, those who wish to convey significant visions would be wise to employ the use of charisma as much as possible in communicating a vision to their followers.

CONVICTION. A final element that enhances the communication of the dream through a verbal message is conviction. The speaker must believe strongly and genuinely in what he says. Kouzes and Posner write, "The greatest inhibitor to enlisting others in a common vision is lack of personal conviction."[5] A speaker will not communicate a vision if he is not convinced of that vision, for his message will ring with the hollow sound of insincerity. People have a way of detecting insincerity, as if they have their ears tuned for it. As stated earlier, trying to cast a vision without personal conviction is like trying to ignite a fire with a wet match.

Speakers who are convinced of their dreams are enthusiastic, committed, and motivated, with the result that they are genuine and expressive in their communication. They come across as people on a mission who speak straight from the heart. They view the podium as an ideal opportunity to expose, convince, and win hearers to their dream or point of view. Even more, they are convinced that their mission is that which is best for those in their audience. They sincerely care about and want the very best for their people, which is the realization of their vision.

A compelling vision provides direction for the message and the energy or drive to move both the speaker and the people in that direction. Visionary speakers have a way of understanding and viewing their sermon topics in the context of the overarching mission. The majority of their messages will present those topics in compelling ways that ultimately point back to the vision. The vision casts a long shadow which encompasses and influences most if not all of the visionary speaker's messages.

At the same time, the vision supplies the visionary speaker with the energy necessary to communicate that vision powerfully and effectively. But where does the dream find its energy? I believe that at least in part the energy is derived from the conviction underlying the vision. That energy is directly proportionate to the extent to which the visionary is convinced of his dream. The stronger the conviction, the stronger will be the vision. Of course, good visions are from God and are based on biblical truth, but not all leaders are equally convinced and moved by that truth. Usually, men and women of strong vision have experienced the life-changing power of biblical truth at some point of difficulty in their lives and, as a result, have come away with deep, abiding convictions. It is these convictions, then, that serve to fuel a lasting fire underneath their vision.

There are numerous examples of sermons or messages that communicate vision. I encourage speakers to study them and to look specifically for examples of the five elements presented above. Vision-sermons are found in Scripture. For example, in Exodus 3:4–10 God communicates to Moses his vision to free his people, Israel, from Egyptian bondage and place them in a prosperous land he has prepared specifically for them. There they will be able to serve him and cast his name among the pagan nations. In Joshua 1:1–9 the same vision is recast before Joshua as the nation of Israel stands on the brink of crossing into the promised land. Finally, Nehemiah's message is found in Nehemiah 2:17, 18. A limiting factor in studying this vision is that he chose to record only the bare essentials of the message. However, several of the elements are present such as an understanding of his audience, positive language, charisma, and conviction.

Many messages from the twentieth century communicate significant visions. These can be helpful because they are somewhat recent and contemporary to the culture. A classic is the "I Have a Dream" sermon preached by Dr. Martin Luther King, Jr., on the steps of the Lincoln Memorial in Washington, D.C., on August 28, 1963. While it was addressed to approximately 250,000 people who were predominantly black, it touched the conscience of the nation and moved the country forward in civil rights for minorities.

Other classics are presidential inaugural speeches. When a new president enters office he communicates his vision for the country through his inaugural address. An example was President John F. Kennedy who, when he assumed the presidency in 1961, said, "And so, my fellow Americans, ask not what your country can do for you; ask what you can do for your country." He inspired a new generation to social conscience and service. Another is President Franklin Roosevelt's first inaugural speech during the Depression (1933) when he said, "The only thing we have to fear is fear itself."

I encourage speakers to study and collect sermons and speeches on vision, whether written or on audio or video cassette. A number are available in books such as *The World's Great Speeches,* which is found in most public libraries and contains numerous speeches classified into various categories according to when, where, and why they were written. While it is possible to create all one's own sermons, it is important to good dream conveyance to be aware of what others are saying and how they are saying it. Their contents and delivery will serve to spark thinking and provide examples and ideas for long-term vision conveyance.

Visual Images

Third, visual images communicate the vision. The idea here is to develop images that when explained remind people of the ministry's vision. They function in the same manner as the vision slogan, which was discussed in chapter 4, only the vision slogan is an auditory device to remind followers of the vision, whereas the image is a visual device to accomplish the same purpose. Both devices are intended not to communicate the vision by themselves but to call attention to a dream that has previously been communicated. The value of using many different devices to convey the vision, as mentioned earlier in this chapter, becomes even more evident here in light of the human capacity to absorb a message through both the ears (as with a slogan or a sermon) and the eyes (as with an image) as well as the other senses.

Following are descriptions of several good examples of visual images.

SLIDE-TAPE PRESENTATION. The slide-tape presentation is a highly effective audiovisual technique that combines a sound track, consisting of either a song or a prepared text, with a series of slides, which can focus on any number of objects such as people, places, or events. For example, I use a slide-tape presentation to communicate a vision in a church planting class I teach at Dallas Theological Seminary. In this course, I attempt to help students catch the vision for planting churches that target and reach nonchurched people. The presentation includes a series of slides which focus on lost, needy people around the world accompanied by a contemporary Christian song entitled "Jesus Saves," which is written and sung by Dallas Holm.

There are, however, at least two problems with using a slide-tape presentation. First, the project takes a significant amount of time to prepare well: taking the photographs and having them developed, choosing the best, and coordinating them with a sound track.

Second, the project will cost some money. Obviously some cost is incurred for the slides. Further is the need to purchase or rent equipment such as a slide projector. If a popular Christian song is used in the sound track, permission must be secured, and there often is a charge, which in my experience has not been significant. If these appear discouraging, keep in mind that the benefits outweigh the disadvantages.

Actually there are some ways to alleviate these problems. The presenter will not have the time to prepare this on his own. Most likely someone in the ministry organization who is gifted and enjoys working with audio-visual techniques can do it. This provides an excellent ministry for someone in a church, possibly a young person, who has not found another outlet for these special, technical talents and abilities. The only caution here is to make sure they truly are talented in these areas. In addition, planning only one of these each quarter gives the production people sufficient time to be ready and to produce a quality piece of work.

There are also some ways to keep costs to a minimum. Someone in the organization may be willing to help defray the cost. In a local church ministry there may be someone who sees the value of this kind of production and would take this on as a personal ministry investment. The people who actually do the production work may decide to invest their finances as well as their time. It should be kept in mind that, outside the purchase of equipment such as a slide projector, the costs are usually minimal.

WELL-DESIGNED LOGO. Another good visual image is a well-designed logo. This has several advantages. Unless an advertising agency or an artist is hired for the job, there is little or no cost in designing and producing the logo.[6] There may be people "in house" who have the artistic abilities to do the design work for the ministry. Clip-art books are available in most bookstores. They provide logo-type figures that may be used directly or adapted to a particular situation.

Another advantage to the logo is that little of the leader's time is required—only when the design for the logo is initially developed, (whether the leader does his own design work or presents the vision and his ideas to the artist), and

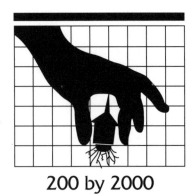

200 by 2000

Figure 1

when the artist's proposed designs are reviewed. Also, little time is required by the viewer of the logo, perhaps only a glance. Although not extensive, the slide-tape presentation requires enough time to be viewed and heard. The logo requires only enough time to be spotted and registered in a person's mind.

A third advantage is that the logo most often can be easily combined with a short vision slogan. For example, as explained in chapter 4, my vision slogan is "200 by 2000." I have placed this slogan under my vision logo (figure 1). This provides two visual stimuli to help people recall the ministry dream, the logo which recalls the vision, and the slogan which reinforces the same vision.

A fourth advantage is that there are many uses for the logo in a church or parachurch ministry. It can be placed on letterheads, memos, signs, newsletters, advertising, bulletins, vehicles, products, music slides, hymnals, and so on. Consequently, people are exposed to the dream in multiple ways through the logo by itself. It is also possible that an organization could design one logo that reflects its over-arching vision. Then it could design other logos that are similar in some way to the initial vision logo but are unique and specifically designed to represent the various ministries within the organization such as evangelism, small groups, discipleship, and others. An excellent example of this is found in the section below, which discusses the use of tapestries as a visual image.

LAPEL PIN. A third visual image is a lapel pin. This technique is not new to Christian ministry. I can recall from the past when various ministry organizations affixed fish hooks or the *ichthus* symbol to a lapel pin. These served various purposes. The *ichthus* symbol, as in the first century, visually identifies the wearer as a Christian. The fish hook gets the attention of a non-Christian, and his question about what it is initiates a conversation about Christ. The hook indicates that the wearer is a "fisher of men," Jesus' words in Matthew 4:19. This pin provides "fishers of men" the opportunity to both answer the question and sow the gospel in the questioner's life.

I suggest attaching the vision logo to a lapel pin. This advertises and identifies the wearer with a particular Christian ministry. It also provides opportunities to share one's faith when people inquire about the nature of the pin. Finally, it serves as a regular visual reminder of the ministry's vision.

TAPESTRY. A fourth visual image is a tapestry or banner. A tapestry is a long, woven ornamental piece of material which may be hung on a wall much like a picture. A symbol or logo can be sewn into the tapestry or a series of tapestries which are then prominently displayed. In the church, the tapestry could be hung at the front of the sanctuary or in the narthex.

An example of a church which uses this method is Fellowship Bible Church of Park Cities located in Dallas, Texas. The church communicates its vision through the use of two doves located next to each other but positioned to face in different directions. The vision consists of "outreach" (evangelism), "upreach" (worship), and "inreach" (edification), each of which is represented by the two doves. The ministry of evangelism is represented by the two doves turned away from each other and facing outward. The ministry of worship is represented by the two doves looking up, and the ministry of edification by the doves facing inward toward each other. Each ministry is represented on a separate tapestry (figure 2). These three tapestries hang at the front of the church. The same designs also appear on the bulletins, stationery, and other appropriate places as logos. If a particular item concerns the worship ministry, such as a music slide or a letter from the music director, then the worship logo appears on it. The same holds true for items associated with the other ministries.

Programs

That programs convey the vision is a subtle truth which applies primarily to local church ministries. The ministries that actually take place in the church communicate the

UPREACH

Worship

INREACH

Edification

OUTREACH

Evangelism

Figure 2

vision of that church regardless of what the church communicates in a vision statement. In short, what you see is what you get. Most churches would agree that their vision is the Great Commission. There are few if any who would vote against evangelism or discipleship. In other circles that would be tantamount to voting against baseball, hot dogs, and apple pie.

However, a quick survey across the American church scene reveals that many churches emphasize one particular area of ministry often at the expense of others. The way to detect this is by looking at their programs. Programming is the litmus test of vision. What a church believes it is doing and actually is doing can be measured by an examination of its programs. For example, some churches emphasize teaching the Bible and the importance of Bible knowledge but do very little evangelism. These churches emphasize teaching in all their programs. Sunday morning begins with Sunday school programs designed to teach children, through adults, the Bible. The Sunday school hour is followed by a morning worship service that concentrates on the sermon, which is a Bible lesson taught by a pastor with the gift of teaching. There is little if any worship. These churches are strongly in favor of evangelism. In fact, the pastor will teach a series of lessons on evangelism at some point during the year, and he will encourage his people to win souls for Christ. But little evangelism takes place, because it is not a part of the program.

Others emphasize evangelism and the importance of winning people for the Savior but are weak in their knowledge of the Scriptures. These churches emphasize evangelism in all their programs. For example, both the Sunday school hour and the morning worship time are used as opportunities for evangelism. The preachers serve as evangelists, and the people are to invite nonchurched neighbors to the service. These churches are all for worship, discipleship, and Bible knowledge. There are even certain times of the year when the pastor emphasizes their importance from the pulpit. But these are not taking place in the church, because they are not a part of the program.

While both of these churches represent the extremes and not the norm, the point is that the church's vision is reflected in the church's programs, and what is important is that everyone knows it. Consequently, an appeal for evangelism in a strong Bible teaching church or an appeal for more teaching in an evangelistic church falls on deaf ears.

There may be a way to correct this problem, but it depends on how willing the church is to change. Churches need to develop their programming around their strategy to accomplish Christ's Great Commission. For example, all people can be found at one of three levels. Level one consists of non-Christians ranging from those who are seekers to those who have no interest in spiritual things. Level two consists of believers who are immature and have not committed themselves to Christ. Level three consists of mature believers who are strongly committed to Christ.

The church's strategy to accomplish the Savior's mission is to move people up these three levels. First, it seeks to move those who are at level one (non-Christian) to level two (salvation) and eventually to level three (maturity). Second, it seeks to move those who are at level two (the immature) to level three (maturity).

To implement this strategy the church must have biblical, culturally relevant programs at each level. To move people from level one to level two (conversion) the church must have evangelistic programs or it will not happen. The same is true regarding discipleship programs for moving people from level two to level three (maturity).

Skits and Drama

Skits and drama are most effective methods for communicating the vision in a church. The church of Jesus Christ in its various forms has known this and practiced it to some degree from the first century through the twentieth century.

Drama can be found in some of the more culturally traditional evangelical churches of the twentieth century, but it tends to be used sparingly outside of Easter and Christmas. In these churches it most often focuses on either an Old or New Testament narrative. When it is used, the actors and actresses dress according to the culture of the original biblical story and the set is designed much the same. Because these presentations require lots of time to tell their story, the entire service plus some additional time is set aside for the presentation. This takes so much effort that people understandably are slow to want to attempt it more than once or twice a year.

However, drama has played an increasingly important role in many of the more culturally contemporary evangelical churches of the late twentieth century and may play an even greater role in the twenty-first century. These churches have taken a different approach. Most of them limit their dramas to less than ten minutes, which allows for other worship elements and a sermon. Some use the drama every Sunday not so much to re-enact a biblical narrative as to create a need to listen to the sermon which follows. Others may use it once or twice a month to communicate a biblical message that may be separate from or similar to that of the sermon. They are not limited to biblical narratives but may focus on biblical concepts found anywhere in the Old or New Testaments.

Also, these churches as a whole have taken a more contemporary approach in their presentations. For example, they will take biblical truth revealed in the first century and apply it to life and problems in the twentieth century. To accomplish this the actors and actresses most often dress in contemporary clothing. I observed an Easter play in one church that lasted only ten minutes. The biblical characters were moved into the twentieth century. Judas became a contemporary business-man, and Mary Magdalene had all the problems of a single woman trying to cope with life in the nineties. The audience in that church on Easter morning, which included many non-Christians, was held spellbound.

Drama has become such an effective medium that churches which desire to exert a strong influence in the twenty-first century should consider its regular use in their ministries. The more contemporary emphasis requires little financial outlay and much less consumption of a person's time or disruption of the church's services. Even in the smaller churches there are usually several people, especially among the youth, who are talented and enjoy writing and producing minidramas. Indeed, it can provide a welcome ministry outlet for those in the church who have not found their place in the other ministries of the church.

Such drama teams can be used most effectively to cast the church's vision. If, indeed, the drama team was formed and used only to convey the vision, it would be worth the time and effort. In most cases, it takes little or no time away from the pastoral staff, and often a good minidrama catches people's attention in ways a sermon cannot. Also, people in your church with abilities in the area of the arts are usually highly creative. They can think of numerous, unique ways to communicate the church's dream through drama and other media as well. Consequently, churches that overlook what has been a seldom used art form do themselves a great injustice in terms of communicating their vision to today's contemporary audience.

The Newcomer's Class

Another good opportunity to convey the vision is in a newcomer's class. This concept can be used effectively in both the church and parachurch ministries. Most older, traditional churches have conducted new members' classes from their inception. These classes may consist of a variety of subjects ranging from the church's history to its doctrinal statement and constitution.

Some of the more contemporary evangelical churches have dropped this practice, because many of them no longer embrace a formal membership. There are several reasons for this. First, many unbelievers have based their eternal standing before God on their membership in a church and not on salvation by grace through faith in Christ. Second, the concept of membership is not found in the Bible and apparently was not necessary in the early church. Finally, membership over the years has in some churches created an artificial barrier between the church's members and regular attenders resulting in an "us" and "them" mentality.

I would encourage the concept of a membership, but I would handle it differently from in the past. First, it must be clear that formal church membership, while not necessarily biblical, is all about commitment, not salvation. When a person joins a church, in effect a twofold commitment takes place. To begin with, the individual makes the strongest of commitments to that church, its programs, and its people and signals that he or she is ready to take a more active role in the life of the church. This has the added advantage of letting the church know who is "on board" and who is not. Second, the church, in turn, makes a strong commitment to the new members as well. This is a commitment to pray for and minister to them in a variety of ways.

I would also change the name of the class from New Members to Newcomers. New people sense the commitment which the term *membership* implies and tend to resist anything associated with it until they are ready to make a strong commitment to the church. Others tend to be reluctant to commit themselves to anything; they find the concept rather frightening. The disadvantage in either situation is that both groups fail to understand what the church is all about and are not integrated into its life in such a way that they grow to maturity in Christ.

The term *newcomers* is a gentler term. It implies that a person can come and "check us out" or find out what we are all about without having to sign, stand, sing, or even say anything. This class can be followed by a nonpressured invitation to formal membership for those who are ready to take this step of commitment.

Also, a clear advantage to having a class for these people, regardless of what it is called, is that some are past the curious state and are ready to move on in their relationship with Christ. If the class is handled properly, these people can find a new dimension in their walk with and commitment to Christ. In short, they have come to a place in their lives where they are ready to make what could be the strongest of commitments to Christ.

Therefore, the newcomers' class or even a new members' class is an excellent time to cast the church's vision. People are either curious about the church or are ready to make a strong commitment to Christ and his church. Either way, they must know what the church is all about and in what direction the church is heading. Those who are merely curious may discover that at this time in their lives they are moving in a different direction. This is important, because that knowledge may spare both them and the church a lot of grief later on.

Those who are ready to commit themselves to the church must know what it is they are committing themselves to. They need to understand where the church is going so they can "get on board" and move with it rather than risk the potential of misunderstanding the vision and later on the possibility of moving against it. Also, the fact that God has been working in their lives and brought them to a point of high commitment is an ideal time for the church to secure the strongest of commitments to the vision.

This is true as well for parachurch ministries. Usually those who are joining them are also at a high point of commitment, probably much higher than those joining a church. This is because they are investing their lives in the ministry; they will serve not just on the weekends but five to seven days a week. Consequently, any parachurch organization should use this entry level time to cast and secure the strongest of commitments to their vision. If the potential employees or members do not understand or are not comfortable with the ministry's vision, they should seek a better "fit."

The State of the Ministry Speech

Once every year in January the President of the United States delivers a State of the Union address. The basic purpose is to summarize the progress his administration has made in the attempt to accomplish his vision for the nation, which, most likely, was announced at his inaugural. A church or parachurch organization could use this same vehicle at the same time of the year to recast and reclarify its vision.

In a parachurch organization, this opportunity could be called the president's state of the ministry address. The organization could set aside this time every year to communicate to its members or employees the overall progress they have made toward the accomplishment of the mission. Some find our president's address a bit boring and filled with needless political rhetoric. In parachurch ministries that strongly emphasize a profound, significant vision of the future, the people who comprise the ministry community will not be bored, because they want to know how they are doing. They are committed to the vision, and they desire to be regularly updated regarding their progress toward the realization of that vision.

In a church ministry, this opportunity could be called the pastor's state of the church sermon. The pastor could do this in two different but important contexts. In a larger church, the first could be to the staff, and the address might be more specific and detailed about particular areas that matter to them. The other would be to the church in general and might be less specific.

A Brochure

A well-designed brochure communicates the vision of both church and parachurch ministries. Within the past few years a large number of ministries and the church in particular have seen the value of producing an informational brochure. This is important in an age of information where the public demands to know something about a church or a ministry before they will frequent it.

Over the years I have collected a number of brochures, most of which come from churches. Their contents provide a wide range of information about the organization. Of course, all give the name, location, and phone number of the ministry. Most identify the pastoral staff, or at least the senior pastor, and include a simple map. From that point, there is wide divergence depending on the nature of the ministry.

Some brochures are developed for new church starts. In addition to the data above, they contain information primarily for those who would make up the initial core group or have an interest in supporting the church financially. The idea is to anticipate the kinds of questions these people might have. A number of brochures will in some way ask and answer the following three questions.

First, they answer the question, Why are we planting a church? The purpose is to present the need for a new church. This is especially appropriate in an area of the country where there are already a significant number of churches such as in the South. Answers to this question usually present the church planter's vision, values, pertinent demographic information, and the specific needs of the community.

Second, many brochures answer the question, What kind of church will we plant? The purpose in answering this question is to explain what ministries the church has to offer and how it is unique compared with other churches in the same area. Most answers discuss such topics as worship, lay ministry, cultural relevance, small groups, and evangelism.

Third, these brochures answer the question, How will we plant this church? The answer usually discusses the church's strategy, which consists of prayer, friendship evangelism, seekers' Bible studies in homes, and plans for financial support.

Some church planters will take a slightly different approach. First, they describe the need for their church in a particular area. Usually this consists of pertinent demographics that point to spiritual needs. Next, they present their vision as the solution to those needs. Most often this is a statement of the Great Commission. Finally, some include their strategy or specific steps they plan to take to implement the vision.

A number of brochures have been developed for established churches. These generally serve to attract visitors and apprise potential members of what the church is all about. They usually contain such information as the church's history, a doctrinal statement, information about the services, a brief letter from the pastor, and the various programs the church offers for its people and the community. One very creative denominational church does all the above, but has enlarged its brochure to include a helpful map of the community, a community profile, and the addresses and phone numbers of several helpful agencies, businesses, and schools. They have targeted this attractive brochure to those people who have recently moved into the area and might be interested in spiritual things in general or a new church home in particular.

Most parachurch ministries have discovered and have been using brochures longer than has the church. In many cases, this is because they have had to communicate to survive. This is especially true for schools and colleges that rely on the dissemination of information to recruit students. Because there are so many diverse parachurch ministries, I hesitate to describe all the different brochures along with their contents.

Certainly, the informational brochure provides an excellent medium through which a ministry can convey its vision. However, in comparing the different church and parachurch ministries, I was surprised to discover that a large number did not include vision statements in their brochures. This was predominantly true of established church ministries. They seemed to include everything but their vision. However, most new church starts made a point of communicating and explaining their visions; indeed, that seemed to be a primary purpose for producing the brochures.

A Song

The production of a special song or music can communicate the vision. While this method applies to some parachurch ministries, it has the greatest potential for use in local church ministries.

This medium has several advantages. Many churches, including some of the smaller ones, have certain gifted people who have the ability to write and produce music. These often untapped persons are usually ready and willing to use their special talents for the ministries of the church. In fact, they would consider this as a part of their ministry. If they happen to be more avant-garde, then this has the added advantage of helping them to find their ministry niche in the local church.

Second, a well-written song could be used extensively in any of the ministries of the church. To help cast the vision, the worship leader could teach the song to the church during a public worship service so that it becomes the vision theme song of the church. After that, it could be worked into formal and informal meetings on almost any occasion, to be sung with or without instrumental accompaniment. Whenever the vision theme song is sung, it will be familiar to the ministry community and serve to cast and recast the vision of the church.

Of course, the song should be done well. It is critical that the words do, in fact, communicate the vision. Also, the musical version needs to be catchy and attractive to the congregation so that they enjoy and even look forward to singing the song. Consequently, the visionary leader may want to work closely with the songwriter in creating the words to the music. Also, if the church does not have anyone with specific abilities in this area, then it may be wise to secure the help of a professional songwriter. Or perhaps one of the current popular or contemporary songs would be sufficient. Then there would be no need to write a new song.

Audio and Videotapes

The American culture has passed through the agricultural and industrial ages and is now progressing at lightning pace through the information age. Tom Peters, the guru of the American marketplace, recently mentioned that he could retreat to his farm quietly nestled in a Connecticut countryside and still remain in contact with practically anyone in any part of the world, because he has a computer, a modem, and a fax machine. While books are still "in," audio- and videotapes are even more "in." One company now offers audiotapes that summarize what is current in books being published on leadership and management in the marketplace so that the business person does not have to take the time to read them. All the person need do is listen to the tape in the car on the way to work or to an appointment.

Of course, there is no good reason why the visionary leader cannot use these same techniques not only to stay abreast of what is taking place in the world of business and management, but to communicate a dream. I have discovered that either an audio- or videotape can be used very effectively to convey dreams. Most cutting-edge twenty-first century ministries are producing both audio- and video-cassettes of how God is using their ministries for the cause of Christ. These are very effective tools for dream casting. For example, Pastor Bill Hybels of Willow Creek Community Church has an audiotape in which he gives his testimony of how reaching nonchurched people became important to him. Consequently, if I desire to seed a vision for reaching the American nonchurched among a selected group of people such as a potential church planting core group or a church board, I will pass around a copy of Pastor Hybels's audiotape. Most listen and catch the vision.

Also, Willow Creek has produced a videotape of one of its seeker services designed to reach nonchurched lost people in the context of a church service on Sunday morning. Either tape can be purchased at a reasonable cost from the church and is well worth the expense.

Other Techniques

There are other means of casting and conveying the vision as well. For example, any ministry could periodically place its vision slogan in a newsletter, brochure, or special bulletin. A ministry could regularly pray and ask others to pray for the realization of the vision. Also, a church could invite individuals to give a testimony which calls attention in some way to the accomplishment of the vision in their lives. Actually, the only limits to various creative ways to communicate a ministry vision are those in the mind of the visionary leader. Consequently, visionary leaders should regularly focus on unleashing their intuitive, creative abilities to come up with new, unique ways to cast the vision.

It must be kept in mind, however, that developing and communicating the vision does not necessarily guarantee the realization of the vision. Another step has to be taken after the initial communication of the dream. This is the implementation of the dream. The next two chapters are designed to explain what is involved in this important process.

6

Overcoming Initial Inertia

Implementing the Vision: Part 1

Between helping Mary with the new baby and trying to carry on an active ministry, Pastor Bob somehow managed to finish reading the book. Actually, it was not that difficult. He merely went without sleep. But that did not seem to deter him. What he had learned was too important to him and the future of his ministry. There was no time to waste. He needed this information now. He believed with all his heart that he had found the answer to his problems at the church.

Though it was a secular book written from a business perspective, Bob was intrigued with all that the book had to say about leadership. The author made a distinction between leadership and management and developed the former concept in detail. Bob had a limited exposure to management. He had learned a few management principles on his jobs, and the one required course on leadership in seminary was, in fact, a course in management. His obvious area of weakness was leadership.

The envisioning aspect of leadership plus such other elements as marketing and quality control were all new to him but made lots of sense. While he did not completely understand all these new concepts, when he applied them to his ministry, they supplied answers to most of the board's questions and many of his own. It was as if a leadership fog had begun to lift.

The board meetings took a new twist. Things changed. He began to meet the questions about leadership with solid answers. The majority of the men were surprised and pleased, he knew, because he could see it on their faces. They were the "hard-chargers." Others, however, appeared perplexed if not somewhat alarmed. He noted that much of what he said went over their heads. He could detect it from their puzzling looks and glassy eyes as he spoke of proactive leadership and taking charge of their future. While some began to look to Bob for leadership, others were hesitant and unsure, and one, Brother Bill, began to argue for their present course of action. As far as he was concerned, they had already implemented all these new ideas. Those who sided with Bob shook their heads in quiet disbelief as Bill spoke. The others merely listened, and a few seemed a little swayed by Bill's rhetoric.

The entire affair came to a head when Pastor Bob returned from his vacation with a clear, compelling direction for the future of the church. He called it a vision, and had developed the slogan, "200 by 2000." His dream was to reach 200 nonchurched people by the year 2000. This was what some had been looking for. These men bought it with only a few suggestions of their own which Bob gladly included. He realized that their ideas were their way of getting their "fingerprints" on the vision. That would be helpful, because some people in the congregation still felt he was a little young and too fresh out of seminary to be their pastor. But they respected the men on the board and would follow an idea if the board endorsed it.

Still others were reluctant to move with Pastor Bob, his new ideas, and his vision for their future. No, this was not the same man they had hired several years earlier, and yes, he had changed. These were good men, but they preferred the status quo. Some told Pastor Bob that he needed to slow down; he was moving too fast. Also, his ideas involved some risk, and while these men were used to taking risks with their own businesses, they were hesitant to do the same with the church or what Brother Bill called "the Lord's business." Finally, after several late night meetings and lots of discussion, these men reluctantly voted to go along with the majority "to keep the peace." Somewhere deep in the resources of his mind, Bob remembered these words: "Men convinced against their will are of the same opinion still." Only one refused to budge.

Pastor Bob and the board began to meet together to develop some creative ways to communicate the vision. Bob referred to them as Vision Casters. Those who were behind the vision liked that. They also had some good ideas gleaned from their marketing experiences as to how they could get the vision "into the hands of the people." He could tell that these men were excited about the possibility of moving the church in a new direction relevant to the 90s, and had been doing a lot of thinking about how to cast the vision.

The men's excitement would have served to fuel Bob's excitement except for the fact that all the men were not on board. There were still those same men who had voted yes with their voices but no in their hearts. Except, that is, for Bill. He let them all know that he was against any new direction for the church, and he was adamant about it. Bill feared change and desperately clung to the past. Over and over again he repeated, "What we've done in the past is good enough for the future. After all, it's gotten us this far, hasn't it?"

Pastor Bob had never been in a situation like this before. He liked the feeling that a number of the men were excited and strongly behind his leadership as they contemplated moving the church in a new direction. But he could not persuade the others to move with them no matter how hard he tried. At times these men came close, and Bob would do what he could to fan the flame. But then Bill spoke up, and promptly doused any hopes of igniting a fire.

Part of the time he felt good; actually, he felt rather excited. But other times he became frustrated, angry, and discouraged. He worried about his reluctant board members. He knew all too well that without their heartfelt support the church would not embrace the new vision. If he were to try to push it through, it might split the church. Those who were behind him detected this as well, and he sensed that their optimism had waned a little.

"Where do we go from here?" The question brought Bob to his senses. He was having breakfast with his most adamant supporter on the board and had begun to daydream over all the recent events. The question startled him. Not only had it interrupted his thoughts, but in what was just a mere flash of time he realized that now for once he knew the answer. It was a good question; no, it was an excellent question, one that had to be answered and acted on if there was to be a future for him at this church.

Assessing the Problem

What Pastor Bob knew was that once the vision was developed and being communicated, the process would not be over. Although it helps immensely, good dream casting by itself does not necessarily result in the implementation of that dream. There yet remains another key step in the all-important envisioning process. The vision has to be implemented. The dream must be transformed into concrete reality. If this step does not take place, then most likely the vision will remain "pie in the sky by and by," a recurring item on a board's monthly agenda.

I believe this transformational step is probably the most difficult aspect of the entire process for two reasons. First, it calls on the visionary leader's interpersonal skills and abilities to work with people in the envisioning process. Some leaders have more expertise here than others. Also, this critical area was not included in Pastor Bob's seminary curriculum. He received no training for interpersonal skills. "After all," Bob said, "they can't cover everything in three years." Second, it is at this point that a leader entrusts the vision to "significant others," as well, for its implementation. Consequently, to a large degree it is out of the visionary's hands and dependent on the commitment, aspirations, and spiritual maturity of people other than himself. The question is, Will these other people carry the ball or fumble the ball? If some are not quick to see the vision or have other agendas, there will be a problem, as Pastor Bob discovered. But there is a solution to this problem. I call it team building.

Presenting the Solution

At this point, some would advise that the solution to Pastor Bob's problem of how to implement his vision would have been good management; that is, he needed to develop a plan. However, this was not the solution here for the simple reason that it takes people to implement any plan. While it is true that Pastor Bob and a number of his men on the board were behind the vision, this was not enough, for it takes a team of people to implement a vision. Pastor Bob did not yet have a full team; too many people were not yet on the same playing field and moving in the same direction. To introduce a plan here would have resulted in a slow, frustrating death for the vision. The reason is that some people would carry through on their planning assignments, while others would do so only halfheartedly or not at all. The solution to this problem, and the leader's number one priority if he is to implement the dream, is to build a team who first owns the same dream.

What Is Team Building?

Team building is the careful, patient construction of a team of people around the organizational vision for the purpose of implementing the vision. Pastor Bob, like so many leaders, had not yet accomplished this. It is true that some were on his team either because they liked him or because they were naturally attracted to his vision. However, when a new leader comes into an established ministry, such as a church, this will not be true of everyone. Some on the board will need more time, for they are by temperament slower decision makers. They want time to think through the vision and its implications for them and the ministry. This should be acceptable unless it turns into procrastination. Most likely, those individuals will own the vision and join the team in time. When this happens the vision will begin to move toward its implementation.

Possibly a large number of people or only one or two individuals will never own the vision. In the former situation, the visionary leader is in trouble. The leader will have to make a critical choice whether to remain and push the vision, which could result in a split in the organization, or move to another ministry. Most likely, the move is the best choice. In the latter, more common situation, where only one or two individuals will not embrace the dream with the rest, it is best to move to implement the vision without their support. The question for them is whether they will go along with the rest or resist the effort to implement the vision. If the answer is the latter, they will need to be dealt with accordingly.

The Role of Leadership in Team Building

Successfully building a team depends primarily on the visionary's leadership skills more than management skills. Contrary to popular opinion, leadership and management are two separate but complementary systems of action. John Kotter summarizes well the difference between the two. He states that leadership is about coping with change, while management is about coping with complexity.[1] At this critical point in the envisioning process, Pastor Bob's problem and that of the reluctant members on his board was coping with change, not complexity. This chapter and the next focuses on the former, and chapter 8 focuses on the latter.

According to Kotter, leadership copes with change through three steps. First, it establishes the direction where a group of people should go, using vision and strategy to chart a clear course through the fog of change. It corresponds with what I have called the development of the vision. Next, leadership communicates that vision to its people and secures their commitment to move in that direction, which Kotter calls alignment. This corresponds roughly with what I call the casting of the vision. However, team building begins at this point in that it attempts to secure a commitment to move with the vision. Finally, leadership energizes people so they will be able to overcome the various obstacles that are sure to surface along the way. Kotter calls this motivation and inspiration.[2] In my process, all of this comes under team building.

In contrast to leadership, Kotter writes, management copes with complexity in three ways. The first is planning and budgeting, which establish goals and the steps necessary to reach those goals and includes allocating the funds to make this happen. The second is organizing and staffing, which means establishing a structure and a set of jobs to accomplish the plan. The third is controlling or monitoring the progress of the plan and solving problems as they surface.[3] This is where Pastor Bob has had some prior training. When he first came to the church he attempted to implement bits and pieces of this part of management, thinking it was what leadership was all about. He had innocently confused management with leadership and substituted management in the place of leadership.

The Two Agendas of Team Building

The visionary leader puts on the helmet of leadership and functions as a player-coach. The kind of team building that implements the vision and wins the game has two agendas. The first agenda is to acquire a commitment from potential players with different interests, backgrounds, ideas, needs, gifts, and abilities to join others who are already on the field and to move together as a team toward the same goal. This was Pastor Bob's most immediate problem. Some of the men on the board had not yet joined the team on the field. They were still sitting on the sidelines

143

trying to understand Bob's direction and wondering if they should play the game Bob's way. Consequently, Pastor Bob had to overcome some initial inertia. This chapter will focus on this agenda.

The second agenda is to help these same people, once they are moving down the field toward the same goal, to overcome various obstacles that are sure to surface as the game progresses. A common fact of life is that nothing progresses as expected. In football, the quarterback may be injured, or the team may run out of downs and face a critical fourth down situation with only inches to go. Since the human fall into sin, life has been full of glitches. What is true of football is true of life in general. The next chapter will focus on this second agenda.

Implementing the Solution

What could help Pastor Bob? How could he craft a team? What practical steps might he take? In the church or parachurch, how does the leader acquire the best players? He must first overcome the initial inertia that surfaces in every situation whether athletics or ministry. There are at least three ways to do so.

The Importance of the Team

No team means ultimately no dream. The reason we quickly forget this is because the people who make up the team have most often taken a back seat to the visionary, which is necessary if he or she is to exercise the leadership necessary to realize the common dream. When we hear of successful ministries, it is usually the leader, not the team, who gets most of the credit.

The team concept is not new to any student of the Scriptures, who knows that New Testament ministry is team ministry. This principle is well illustrated both in the ministries of the Savior and the apostle Paul. It should be kept in mind that their teams were largely responsible for initiating the spread of Christianity around the world, and that twenty centuries later, our faith in Christ can be traced to their teamwork.

Jesus Christ as deity has all authority and power in heaven and on earth (Matt. 28:18). This great truth was regularly celebrated in the Old Testament when the various writers and prophets reminded the people of Israel that their God was the One who created the heavens and earth and all that is in them. In the Gospels, Jesus exercised this awesome power to perform various miracles such as healing the sick and raising the dead. It is important to note that he did not need a band of unimpressive, common laborers to realize his mission, for he could have accomplished it on the spot with only a command from his lips (Matt. 26:53). It could have been a sacred solo performance. Yet, instead of doing it alone, he chose to work through them. Later, the Gospels record, he did much the same when he appointed and sent out seventy others in addition to the apostles (Luke 10).

The apostle Paul did not, of course, have the same power and authority as the Son of God, and he chose not to attempt the Great Commission vision alone, but decided to work through a team effort. Prior to his first church planting journey, the team consisted of Barnabas and Paul (Acts 11:22–30). Then, on the first church planting trip, they added Mark to the team (Acts 13:2, 3, 5). On the second trip, he added Silas (Acts 15:40), Timothy (Acts 16:1–3), Luke (Acts 16), and others (Acts 18). Finally, on the third trip, additional people were either added to the team or used to form new teams. Thus, in Acts 19 and 20 such names appear as Erastus, Gaius, Aristarchus, Sopater, Secundus, Tychicus, and so on. In addition, Paul in some of his letters identifies various individuals who may very well have been important members of his team, such as those mentioned in Romans 16:21–23.

In light of the ministries of Jesus and Paul, there can be little doubt that New Testament ministry was team ministry. Some leaders have proved slow to learn this basic lesson. They become so motivated by the vision that they run far out ahead of their teams and attempt to implement it on their own. They function as a team of one. Pastor Bob was such a leader. However, he reached a point where he understood this truth and purposefully set out to recruit visionary followers for the cause. And he learned it takes time.

Recruiting the Team

Whenever leaders decide to recruit a team to implement the dream, they must ask and answer two questions: Who will make up the team? How will these people be enlisted?

WHO WILL BE ON THE TEAM? The answer depends on the nature of the ministry organization and who are in strategic positions to influence, either positively or negatively, the implementation of the dream.

If that organization is parachurch, then most likely the team will consist of those who make up the immediate ministry community such as the various staff and personnel. If the organization is a local church, then the team will consist of those who are on the ministry staff plus any leadership boards.

However, in both church and parachurch ministries this should be viewed only as a beginning. It is hoped that these people, in turn, will recruit all others who in some way can create coalitions that both understand and are committed to the dream's realization. Consequently, recruitment is everyone's business. The goal is to recruit recruiters and to enlist enlisters. The hope ultimately is to reach anyone who is in a position either to help or even stymie the implementation of the dream.

HOW WILL THEY BE RECRUITED? The primary recruitment tool is the vision or dream itself. Constantly conveying a vision that will meet the audience's basic values, needs, and aspirations will recruit recruits. It is akin to offering a thirsty man a cold drink of water on a hot summer day. Kotter agrees and identifies some of these basics as the need for "achievement, belonging, recognition, self-esteem, a sense of control over one's life, and living up to one's ideals."[4] Most people find it hard to resist a vision that proposes to deliver in these areas of their lives.

This recruitment tool can be used in both planted and established ministries as well. The advantage of using vision casting as a vehicle for recruitment in a new ministry start is the leader's greater capacity to know who is committed to the vision from the very beginning. Usually those who are not committed to the vision will not stay around; they vote with their feet.

In established ministries where there may not be a vision, dream casting will surface those who are thirsty and those who are not. The next step, building the team, should help to win over those who are not thirsty.

Again, the desire is that once these people have enlisted, they, in turn, will enlist others. This is well illustrated by the recruitment that took place among the apostles. In John 1:38 the Savior invited Andrew and another disciple to come and stay with him for a day. Next (vv. 41, 42) Andrew recruits his brother Peter. Again, Jesus recruits Philip (v. 43). Then Philip finds and recruits Nathanael (vv. 45–51). Hopefully, this recruitment process will continue throughout the life of the ministry, especially in the church. There will always be a need for team members. That is another reason for continually keeping the vision before the people's eyes.

Building the Team

Once visionary leaders recognize the importance of the team to their ministry, and then recruit the best team possible, they are finally ready to craft their team into a unit that can accomplish the first agenda. The rest of this chapter consists of two sections. The first discusses the critical elements of commitment and cooperation in constructing a team and how the one affects the other. The second will show how to catalyze the kind of commitment in people that builds strong teams.

THE ELEMENTS OF COMMITMENT AND COOPERATION.

Team building cannot be accomplished without two key ingredients: commitment and cooperation. Remember, Pastor Bob discovered that some of his leaders were committed and cooperating and some were not.

Commitment. Any good coach will affirm the fact that it takes commitment, lots of commitment, to play the game of football. Most who watch a college or professional game on television are not always aware of this, but behind every weekend performance has been an entire week of long, sometimes agonizing practices, not to mention the fact that some players are coping with various nagging injuries.

Most often, the amount of success athletes experience on the field can be measured by the degree of their commitment to the total process both on and off the field. Kotter says that a key ingredient of leadership is getting the team to understand the vision and be committed to its achievement.[5] The degree to which the ministry leadership team accomplishes their vision depends on their willingness to do whatever it takes to get the job done. Without this commitment, the entire envisioning process comes to a frustrating halt.

Cooperation. Also, any good football coach will agree that in addition to commitment, it takes lots of cooperation to win at the game of football. If an offensive lineman decides that he does not want to block for the quarterback when he drops back to pass or for a back when he runs with the ball, the result could be disaster. The implementation of a dream like the game of football depends on mutual cooperation among all the players in the game. The degree to which the team wins or loses depends on their willingness to work together.

At the same time most people acknowledge that cooperation is not easy. However, people who work together under the same dream are more inclined toward ensuring one another's success. Mutual cooperation replaces mutual competition. People are free to use their God-given talents and abilities, which brings success. The success of one member of the team means the success of all the members of the team. In their book entitled *The Leadership Challenge* Kouzes and Posner write: "Fostering collaboration is not just a nice idea. It is the key that leaders use to unlock the energies and talents available in their organizations. . . . Leaders realize that the key to doing well lies not in competition or in overcoming others but in gaining their cooperation."[6]

Commitment affects cooperation. Whether the sport of football or the field of ministry, this kind of cooperation is the fruit of commitment. Cooperation is the result of commitment. The degree of cooperation is directly proportional to the degree of commitment. The higher the commitment to the dream, the higher will be the cooperation to achieve that dream. Therefore, the leader who is able to enlist the commitment of his people will, most likely, also gain the cooperation of his people, and the result is strong teams. In a sense, the issue then is commitment. If somehow Pastor Bob could win the commitment of his reluctant board members, he would gain their cooperation as well, with the result that he would have an empowered team that would realize the same compelling vision for their future. But how might he win a heart commitment from his entire team?

CATALYZING COMMITMENT IN A POTENTIAL TEAM. Four ways leaders can build commitment in their people are the constant casting of the vision, creating a climate of trust and vulnerability, developing a sense of community spirit, and maintaining clear lines of communication.

First, when a well-designed vision articulates a positive, dynamic picture of the future and addresses the people's needs, when people are recruited for the team they are willing to commit themselves to that team.

When Pastor Bob returned from his vacation with a powerful, significant vision for the church, his supporters on the board were "hooked." This was what they had been waiting for; the dream represented the missing piece to the puzzle. At that point, they joined Pastor Bob's team and made the necessary commitment to accomplish the dream, even though the other board members had not caught the vision. Commitment cultivated by the vision affects cooperation. A problem that constantly plagues team building is the mutual rivalry which sometimes erupts between team members who have different gifts and abilities. Most people believe that other people are just like them, that they think and see the world through the same set of glasses and share the same talents and passions. Consequently, when others behave or think differently, people become critical of them, which fosters competition instead of cooperation. The apostle Paul addresses this in 1 Corinthians 12:17–20:

> If the whole body were an eye, where would the hearing be? If the whole were hearing, where would the sense of smell be? But now God has placed the members, each one of them, in the body, just as He desired. And if they were all one member, where would the body be? But now there are many members, but one body.

However, when all share a deep commitment to the same dream, they begin to realize that it takes people with different but complementary gifts, talents, and abilities to accomplish that dream. One person on the team realizes that he or she needs the other persons if anything of significance is to be accomplished for the Savior, and members value and appreciate how God has designed each one differently so that all can, in fact, realize what they desire. Team members acknowledge that without each other success would not have happened. The potential for destructive competition is eliminated and replaced by mutual cooperation.

Second, people who implicitly trust one another work well together. They foster mutual cooperation toward reaching group goals. Those who do not trust one another accomplish little, which signals an early funeral for most teams. Obviously Pastor Bob's backers on the board had confidence in him and the new direction of the church, while other board members did not share this same confidence. As long as they continued to withhold their trust it would affect the future of the vision and the future of the board as well. Eventually something would have to give. Either Pastor Bob would leave the church or some of the board members would leave the board and possibly the church.

Lack of trust was the major factor in the dissolution of the Paul–Barnabas team in Acts 15:37–40. At issue was the credibility of a former team member, John Mark, who, according to verse 38, had deserted them in a prior ministry situation in Pamphylia. In light of this breach of confidence, Paul believed that John Mark could not be trusted in future ministry situations. Barnabas disagreed and believed they should give the man another chance. Trust was such an important issue to these men that they decided to part company, form separate teams, and go their separate ways.

There are several ways to cultivate a climate of trust. To begin, the leader must set the example. If he expects people on the team to trust one another, then it is imperative that he trust them. Perhaps this was Barnabas's thinking in giving John Mark a second chance. A good rule of thumb is to trust people until they give you a reason not to. This may have been the factor in Paul's rejection of John Mark.

This does not mean, by the way, that people have to always agree with one another. For example, there is not a person on the faculty at Dallas Seminary whom I do not trust. In fact, I would trust any faculty person with my life. I suspect that they feel the same way toward me. At the same time, this does not mean that we always agree. However, our mutual trust creates an environment in which we as a faculty team can resolve our differences, love one another, and accomplish our vision as an institution.

Another way to cultivate trust is to delegate responsibilities, also a way of modeling trust. We see this in the example of the Savior when he delegated ministry to the disciples as in Matthew 10 and to the seventy in Luke 10.

A leader cultivates trust when he is open and thus vulnerable to people on the team. His willingness to share his deepest fears or greatest shortcomings with others communicates that he trusts them and grants them a certain degree of integrity. They are thereby encouraged to be similarly open and honest. I suspect that in Pastor Bob's tenure at the church he had spent very little time alone with each of his reluctant board members in a posture of vulnerability.

Leaders also develop trust when they encourage others to participate in decision making, especially when it relates to their areas of expertise. For example, when my departmental team at Dallas Seminary meets together, one of the members may raise an issue that calls for a decision. My response is to ask what this particular member recommends we do, since this lies within his area of ministry expertise. Very rarely do we not follow that recommendation. This communicates loudly our faith in him and his abilities to lead and manage with sustained excellence.

Third, develop a sense that all on the same team are part of the same community, thereby imparting a sense of togetherness. This is not *my* ministry, it is *our* ministry; this is not *my* dream, it is *our* dream. Use the pronoun *we* rather than *I*, or *our* rather than *my*. Kouzes and Posner suggest this in *The Leadership Challenge:*

> *Always say we.* When thinking and talking about what you plan to accomplish and have accomplished, it is essential that you think and talk in terms of *our* goals. Your task as a leader is to help other people to reach mutual goals, not your goals. You never accomplish anything alone, so your attitude can never be "here's what I did" but rather "here's what we did." This language reinforces the belief that goals are truly collaborative, not exploitative.[7]

It is instructive to trace the use of these pronouns, through the Book of Acts, by the various teams of Peter and John (Acts 4:20), the apostles (Acts 5:29), Paul and Barnabas (Acts 15:36), and others.

Another way to develop a sense of community or team spirit is by spending time together. This makes it possible for people to get to know each other beyond the normal daily office or monthly board routines. The better you know other people, the better you understand them and their various circumstances in life. This helps to discern why they do the things they do, whether good or bad. This concept is not without excellent precedent. Jesus chose to spend time with the twelve disciples. It is recorded in Mark 3:14 that "He appointed twelve, that they might be with Him, and that He might send them out to preach." Those in the early church spent time together in fellowship and small groups (Acts 2:42, 46).

In a church this can be accomplished by frequent board retreats, participation in small groups, visiting in homes, and so on. In a parachurch ministry it can happen through such events as birthday parties, socials, luncheons, and company picnics. The only limit on all the possibilities is one's imagination. Of great value, in particular, is mutual participation in team sporting events such as volleyball, basketball, softball, or golf. This enables people to play together in team situations that are different from those normally experienced at work or the church. The idea is that those who play together stay together.

Fourth, most individuals want to know what is going on. They want to keep abreast of what is taking place in their ministry or workplace. Naisbitt illustrates this from the marketplace when in *Megatrends 2000* he writes:

> People want to know what is going on in their company. In the same Steelcase poll, 76 percent rated "free exchange of information among employees and departments" very important; only 35 percent said it described their office.[8]

Later in the same article, he quotes Everett Sanders, chairman of three Atlanta companies:

> "As time went on, my managers became almost as interested in all facets of the company as I was," he says. People who are kept posted, he says, feel they have a stake in the

company and "work even harder when all is not going well."[9]

If people ever begin to suspect that the leader is hiding something from them, he will lose considerable credibility. Paul urges us to speak the truth in love (Eph. 4:15). Those involved in team ministries deserve to know the truth about what is taking place on the team. The key, as Paul mentions, is to communicate it in love.

It is best to communicate face to face. It is instructive to note that whenever there is conflict between people, Jesus urges them to get together and seek resolution (Matt. 5:23, 24; 18:15–17). One-on-one communication allows people to be open, honest, and emotional if necessary without having to worry about what others will think. The advantage is that if someone has some negative information about another person that is not correct, the situation can be corrected without damaging the person's reputation. Another way to communicate is in a group context as when a leader addresses the team, or several people, in turn, address the team as in Acts 15:6–21; 20:17.

Good communication that builds commitment includes the resolution of any conflicts between people who are on the same team. It goes almost without saying that people will not cooperate with those with whom there has been some kind of unresolved strife. It is common in ministry to hear horror stories about churches where there are board members who frequently skirmish with one another or the pastor because of some unresolved conflict.

Both Matthew 5:23, 24 and Matthew 18:15 urge that conflicts be resolved quickly at the initiative of either the offending or the offended party. The point is: Get it taken care of. The wisdom here is evident, because the longer a problem goes without resolution, the worse it becomes. The importance of resolution is emphasized in Matthew 5:24 where it is given priority over worship.

It is difficult to tell at this point if Pastor Bob had offended anyone on his board, with the possible exception of Brother Bill. The lines of communication were not open between him and his sidelined elders. It was imperative that he go to them and attempt to cultivate a relationship with each of them. If anyone was upset or had been offended, he would find this out rather quickly. Then, in the context of that relationship, he could begin to communicate and help his men understand the vision and why they were essential to the realization of that vision. I suspect that Bob was not too excited about spending any time with Brother Bill. That is not unexpected, because those with whom we disagree the most we avoid the most. But I believe that those with whom we disagree the most we know the least, the likely reason we disagree to begin with. For Bob to do everything in his power to reach out to Brother Bill would provide a powerful model for all the men on the board of the kind of commitment necessary to realize their dream.

Visionary leaders who work hard at building commitment and cooperation in their people will empower teams that work together toward a positive, significant dream for the future. This accomplishes the first agenda of team building. However, that same team will run headlong into various obstacles on the way toward the realization of their dream. Overcoming them is the second agenda of team building, the topic of the next chapter.

7

Overcoming Obstinate Obstacles

Implementing the Vision: Part 2

As a developing leader, Pastor Bob was a young man of action and integrity. As soon as he had read about the three principles of team building, he took action to apply them to his sidelined board members. When he initially attempted to implement the vision, he had assumed that it would be a team effort—a team, that is, in the sense that the board would go along with his vision and let him "do his thing." The reluctance of some changed his attitude toward their role and their importance as a team. He had not thought a lot about recruiting a team, because he inherited one, the board, when he agreed to become the pastor of the church. Supposedly, a team was already in place. When some of the board did not respond, he realized the need to recruit them and re-form a new team in line with the new vision. Finally, he benefitted most from the application of the team building principles, as we will see shortly.

Pastor Bob took quick action not only for the sake of the vision but also because he craved a better relationship with these men. In his own personal devotional life he was cultivating a strong passion and love for the Savior, which had begun to affect his attitude toward the men. He was growing in his love for them and began to view each in a different light. He no longer saw them as mere objects to be used in realizing the vision but as talented men with good hearts, and he valued their presence on the board.

Several months had passed and there had been a definite thaw in their relationships. Pastor Bob had begun to spend time with each man on a personal basis. They would get together for an early breakfast or a quick lunch. There would be some time for practical, relevant Bible study and intense personal prayer. As Bob opened up to the men, they opened up to him. He was not aware of some of the difficulties these men faced in their lives. He prayed with one man about the business ethics of his boss. There was going to be a confrontation, and it might cost him his job at a time when jobs were scarce in his field. He prayed with another over a child who had all the symptoms of multiple sclerosis. He prayed again with one whose business was going "down the tubes," and there was a grandchild born with Down syndrome.

Pastor Bob also found himself asking some men for their forgiveness. While he had not intentionally meant to offend anyone, some of his jokes had fallen on sensitive ears. He should have been more alert to the ethnic origins of a few of the men. In other cases, it was not so much what he said but the way he said it. One man actually felt that an entire sermon was purposefully directed at him. Some of the issues seemed a little petty, but he swallowed his pride and did what he knew was best without violating his personal integrity. To his amazement some of the men came to him and asked his forgiveness for their attitudes toward him. One man confessed that he had transferred to Bob his anger toward the former pastor who, he felt, had abandoned them for bigger and better things.

Gradually Bob's empty social calendar began to fill up with various invitations from the men on the board. He learned how to fish for largemouth bass and actually went skiing for the first time. He attended several professional ball games and became a fan of the local team who were affectionately nicknamed "The Mighty Mud Hens." In all this flurry of activity, Bob's waistline grew an inch due to the culinary abilities of some of the men and their wives. But that would be taken care of shortly, because he had begun to jog in the mornings with a man on the board. He also noticed that when they introduced him to their friends, they referred to him as "my pastor" not "the pastor" as they had done in the past.

In the midst of all this activity, he had decided not to say as much about the vision, but in time some of the men brought it up on their own. They had begun to see a need for some changes. The church had plateaued in its growth while the community was growing at a phenomenal rate. Something must be wrong. Some had begun to dream on their own and wanted to know more about "200 by 2000." Their questions and responses hinted at a growing trust in his leadership. If it was important to Pastor Bob, well, now it was important to them.

Brother Bill still maintained a certain distance from Pastor Bob. While Bob's relationship had improved with the other men on the board, things were much the same with Bill if not a little worse. Bob had gone to Bill on several occasions and extended the olive branch, with little response. Most of the men were aware of Bob's actions and applauded him for his efforts. Several acknowledged that for them this was a turning point in their feelings about Bob's leadership and the direction of the church.

Brother Bill continued to participate on the board but increasingly assumed an adversarial role. He did not appear to vote for much of anything except to maintain the status quo, which one of the board in private ardently claimed was Latin for "the mess we're in." The rest did not know Latin, so there was no debate. Brother Bill was against change, did not see a need for it, he claimed. Others believed that he was frightened by the concept. He regularly reminded everyone of the "good old days" when the church was first planted and everybody knew everybody. As far as he was concerned, the church was too big, and he did not want to see it grow any bigger.

As the months passed, increasing attention was given to the vision. Most of the men had voluntarily left the sidelines and joined the team. Furthermore, they appeared to be moving down the field together toward the same goal, "200 by 2000." They were genuinely excited about the idea of reaching 200 nonchurched people by the year 2000. However, there was general agreement that Pastor Bob had set the figure too low; they could do better than that. Perhaps they should change the vision slogan to "2000 by 2000," especially in light of all the young couples who had recently moved into the community along with a growing number of singles and single parent families.

However, various obstacles began to surface. Bob referred to them privately as his obstinate obstacles. There was the ever-present problem of Brother Bill. Some of Pastor Bob's most adamant supporters had grown weary of listening to Bill's objections as the vision gained momentum. Besides, there were people in the church who listened to Brother Bill. He had a small contingent of vocal followers who, in general, agreed with him. There were parents who were concerned about how bringing a lot of nonchurched families and their kids into the church would affect their own children. For them Sunday school provided a safe haven where their kids could come and be insulated from drugs, alcohol, and people who were addicted to them.

There were other obstinate obstacles as well. Some people objected to the inclusion of contemporary Christian songs in the morning worship service along with the old hymns of the faith. There was also some talk of beginning a band, which might include a drummer. They hoped this was only a false rumor. At the same time, the young couples in the church loved it and had begun inviting some of their friends. If this kept up, they would be faced with starting a second morning service.

Still there was another group, rather small in size, who were most concerned with what they believed was a growing lack of emphasis on the Bible in the pastor's sermons. They had liked it better when he preached for an hour covering word-for-word a single passage of the Bible. Now he spent too much time talking about how it applies to people's lives from Monday through Sunday. They were also concerned about the fact that he no longer gave an altar call after the sermon. They viewed this as evidence that he had "gone soft" on evangelism.

It would be a mistake to assume that because the men on a team are committed to the organization's vision it is certain to be implemented. The problem is that certain obstacles are sure to surface which have the potential to discourage the team or divert its attention from the dream. This is destined to take place in any ministry organization, whether it is the church or the parachurch. Therefore, we should not be surprised at what took place at Pastor Bob's church.

In the previous chapter I said that team building is necessary to accomplish two agendas. First, it is necessary to craft a team of people who are in a position to influence the vision to move together in the same direction. This is usually accomplished when visionary leaders understand that they cannot accomplish the dream without a team, recruit the team primarily by repeatedly conveying the dream, create a climate of trust and vulnerability by developing a sense of community or team spirit, and keep their lines of communication open.

The second agenda is to craft a ministry team in such a way that people keep moving in the right direction despite various obstinate obstacles that impede their progress. This is accomplished in the fourth and fifth steps of the team building process.

Empowering the Team

The fourth step in building the team is to empower the team. Empowerment is an important concept in leadership. In defining the term for businesses, Conger writes, "Empowerment, then, is essentially a process of strengthening subordinates' convictions in their own self-efficacy."[1] I would redefine the term for leadership in the Christian context as the process of strengthening the team members' beliefs in their abilities to overcome potential vision-blocking obstacles through their resources in Christ. Conger's definition rests solely on various God-given talents and abilities that reside to a certain extent within all people. In general, these are present at birth and may be developed through training. My definition includes Conger's natural gifts and abilities, which are, indeed, from God, but adds the supernatural dimension that every believer has through Christ. These will be explored later.

Conger further explains the importance of empowerment when he writes: "These beliefs are critical because they determine the extent to which people will initiate and persist in attempts to master difficult experiences."[2] The principle is rather simple. If people do not believe they can overcome certain obstacles on the way to accomplishing their goals, then they will fail. This is true regardless of the nature of the obstacle or their personal abilities to cope with them. This explains why some very obviously gifted people fail miserably in life, while those who appear less talented are successful. Whereas some people will avoid situations they mistakenly believe are beyond their abilities, others will attempt the impossible.

The obvious lesson for visionary leadership is that successful leaders help their people to realize their tremendous potential to overcome seemingly impossible tasks. Conger further elaborates:

> In essence, then, empowerment heightens a person's willingness to attempt difficult tasks and to make sustained efforts without necessarily a concern for positive outcomes. Tasks that would have been judged too difficult are now perceived as feasible. Empowerment is critical for charismatic leaders because it allows them to mobilize their organization in the face of monumental challenges. Even though high and sometimes unrealistic expectations may be set by the leader, they will be accepted.[3]

162

Thus, through empowerment, team members will take a more positive approach toward overcoming vision obstacles whether they think they will succeed or not. But how does a visionary leader empower his team to approach obstacles in this manner? There are several ways to accomplish this.

Empowerment through Self-worth

Visionary leaders empower their teams by helping them to recognize their true value and significance in light of the grace of God through Jesus Christ. Many Christians, including seasoned leaders and board members, face a constant struggle with their feelings of self-worth. The problem is that we live in a real world filled with pain, rejection, and failure. The problem-free life is a fiction. Life is a series of problems that make constant assaults on our self-worth. Therefore, when various obstinate obstacles or difficulties challenge, people may or may not respond well depending on their present emotional state. If they are experiencing low esteem, they may give up without firing a shot. If they are feeling good about their worth, they may tackle the problem head on and win.

The answer to this problem is for visionary leaders first to understand for themselves, and then teach their people the doctrine of God's grace and how it affects the Christian's daily life. In Romans 5:2 Paul states that through Jesus Christ "we have obtained our introduction by faith into this grace in which we stand." Not only are we saved by grace through faith (Eph. 2:8, 9), but we are to live by grace each day of our lives. Grace does not take a vacation after the cross. Sounds good, but what does that mean? Even more important, what does it have to do with a Christian's self-esteem?

In his book *The Search for Significance* Robert McGee writes: "Whether labeled 'self-esteem' or 'self-worth,' the feeling of significance is crucial to man's emotional, spiritual, and social stability, and is the driving element within the human spirit. Understanding this single need opens the door to understanding our actions and attitudes."[4] He further points out that our hunger for self-worth is God given and can only be satisfied through a relationship with him. In fact, God in his love for us through the grace of Christ has already met all of our esteem needs.

McGee is a professional Christian counselor and the founder and president of Rapha, a nationally recognized health care organization that provides in-hospital and out-patient care with a Christ-centered perspective for adults and adolescents suffering psychiatric and substance abuse problems. He indicates that through his study of the Scriptures and his counseling interaction with people, he has discovered four obstacles that plague the majority of people in their search for significance.

PERFORMANCE. The first obstacle to a sense of significance is the belief that we must perform and meet certain standards to feel good about ourselves. The symptoms of this belief in our lives are such things as the fear of failure, perfectionism, manipulation, an intense drive or desire for success, and an avoidance of risks. However, we must realize that our value does not depend on our abilities to meet certain standards, whether our own or others', but on what Jesus Christ accomplished at the cross, in particular justification. According to Romans 5:1, we have been justified in God's eyes through faith in Christ. This means that we already have his righteousness or perfection not through what we do but what he has done for us at the cross. The standard has already been met, and we now are fully pleasing to our Father. In effect, to attempt to meet certain standards for our self-worth is fruitless, because the standard has already been met through our justification. We do not need to strive after what we already have. As they say in Texas, "It's a done deal."[5]

ACCEPTANCE. The second obstacle to a sense of significance is the belief that we must be accepted by others to feel significant. The symptoms of this belief in our lives are such things as the fear of rejection, the desire to please others regardless of the cost, an unusual sensitivity to criticism, and withdrawal to avoid criticism. But God, because of his grace in Jesus Christ, has met this problem as well, in particular through reconciliation. According to Colossians 1:21, 22, we have been reconciled to God through the cross of Christ. In Christ we have God's complete and unconditional acceptance. As a result, our acceptance and worth are not dependent on other people, because we are fully pleasing and totally accepted in Christ.[6]

BLAME. The third obstacle to a sense of significance is the belief that when we fail, we are unworthy of love and deserve to be punished. The symptoms of this belief are self-blame, blaming others rather than ourselves when we fail, the fear of punishment, punishing others, and the drive to avoid failure at all costs. The solution is the grace of God in Christ, in particular propitiation. According to 1 John 4:9–11, Jesus Christ became the propitiation or satisfaction for our sins. He satisfied the wrath of God by taking our punishment on himself. Therefore, we no longer have to fear punishment or shift our blame to others, because Christ paid for all of our sins at the cross.[7]

SHAME. The fourth obstacle to a sense of significance is the belief that we are what we are. We cannot change; therefore, we are hopeless. The symptoms are feelings of shame, hopelessness, and inferiority. Also, there may be isolation and withdrawal from others. Again, the solution is God's grace in Christ, in particular regeneration. According to John 3:3–6 and other passages, we have become a new creation in Christ. We have changed because he has imparted new life to us through the cross of Christ. Regeneration is not our work but it is the work of the Holy Spirit who makes each one of us a new person the very moment we trust Christ. We no longer need to feel hopeless, shameful, or inferior, because in Christ we are no longer the people we used to be without Christ.[8]

Ultimately, what we learn from God's loving grace through Jesus Christ is that not only did God provide sufficient grace to save us but that grace continues to operate and liberate us from the various obstacles that seek to demean us and lower our personal worth in our own eyes. Jesus Christ is our single source of security and the only basis for our self-worth.

To understand this divine truth and begin to live accordingly, to grasp their real worth and significance in Christ allows visionary leaders to approach the various obstacles that come into their lives and ministries with a totally different attitude. In whatever they do, it would be nice to have the approval and acceptance of their peers and friends, but when (not if) they do not grant that acceptance and approval, leaders are still unconditionally loved, accepted, and valued by God through Christ. This knowledge is refreshing and liberating and allows Christians to approach leadership with a totally different perspective. They are no longer afraid to tackle ministry-related or personal problems head on, and they take good risks, because their self-worth is not dependent on their success or acceptance by others but on God's unconditional grace in Jesus Christ.

It is imperative that visionary leaders incorporate this truth in their lives, and then, in turn, teach this truth verbally and by example to those who make up their teams. Once leaders have implemented this grace in their lives, they must treat people accordingly. In what they say and do they must value others as persons just as Christ values them. Next, leaders teach the truths of God's grace. In fact, teaching this truth alone has the potential to empower a leadership team so as to accomplish their dream. But there is more.

Empowerment through Personal Confidence

Visionary leaders empower their teams by developing each person's confidence in his or her abilities to be used by God. Not only do Christians struggle with feelings of insignificance, they often tend to demean their individual abilities to handle tasks and obstacles for God. They lack self-confidence. They view themselves as either average or below par in their capacity to be used of God. Therefore, when they encounter obstacles, they often react with low expectations of themselves and little assurance of ministry accomplishment.

While this may not be a constant in their lives, it has a way of periodically cropping up and hindering their pursuit of sustained excellence in their ministries for Christ. Therefore, it is imperative that leaders train and encourage their organizational teams to approach their leadership and ministries with a bold confidence in their God-given abilities. There are several reasons for this.

DIVINE DESIGN. Each Christian has been divinely designed and enabled by God for service. To denigrate our abilities is to denigrate his special design and work in our lives. At birth God uniquely blessed each of us with certain natural talents, abilities, and temperaments to be used for him. At the point of conversion, he added certain God-given spiritual gifts. This affects such areas of our lives as our work, how we learn, and so on.

As long as we operate within that design, we must realize that we can overcome huge obstacles and accomplish great things for God. Rather than denigrate our abilities, we should regularly celebrate our God-given abilities. Consequently, every ministry for Christ, whether church or parachurch, should develop a program of assessment to help its people discover and then properly implement their divine design. This will enable them to come much closer to realizing their full potential for Christ and his ministry.

MINISTRY NICHE. Since God has uniquely designed and gifted all believers, then each has a ministry niche where he or she can excel. The idea here is that every believer is a "ten" somewhere.[9] This truth should lend encouragement to all believers and inspire them not only to discover their design but to become actively involved in their particular ministry area. This enables them to experience all the excitement and benefits that result from ministering with sustained excellence.

DIVINE EMPOWERMENT. We can be confident in our abilities, because God indwells each of us at the point of conversion and empowers those natural abilities to be used for him. Paul asks in 1 Corinthians 6:19, "Or do you not know that your body is a temple of the Holy Spirit who is in you, whom you have from God, and that you are not your own?" This passage teaches an amazing truth of Christianity, which is the fact that God takes up his residence in our lives. One result of his indwelling is our empowerment to act in life. Thus, in Colossians 1:29 Paul could write, "And for this purpose also I labor, striving according to His power, which mightily works within me."

This, in turn, makes it possible for us to accomplish far more than most people realize. I believe that a large number of Christians fail to realize their full potential in Christ, because they are not aware of all that he can accomplish through them as the result of his indwelling and empowering them. An example is the church at Ephesus. To this church Paul wrote: "Now to him who is able to do exceeding abundantly beyond all that we ask or think, according to the power that works within us." He warns that those believers were not thinking and asking big enough, in light of the power of the indwelling Holy Spirit. As a result, they were missing the realization of their full potential for God.

Empowerment through Servant-Leadership

Visionary leaders empower their teams by personally serving their teams. The model for leadership found in the New Testament is that of servant-leadership. Jesus Christ established this model when he led and served his disciples during his ministry on earth. In a discussion of the difference between his leadership and pagan leadership, the Savior says, in Matthew 20:26–28, "It is not so among you, but whoever wishes to become great among you shall be your servant, and whoever wishes to be first among you shall be your slave; just as the Son of Man did not come to be served, but to serve, and to give His life a ransom for many."

It is most important to note that while Christ was on earth, he did not spend all of his time with the multitudes but spent much of his time pouring his life into his disciples. Coleman writes: "He actually spent more time with His disciples than with everybody else in the world put together. He ate with them, slept with them, and talked with them for the most part of His entire active ministry."[10] Coleman further observes: "Contrary to what one might expect, as the ministry of Christ lengthened into the second and third years He gave increasingly more time to the chosen disciples, not less."[11]

In light of the impact the disciples have had on the world, we understand why Jesus spent so much time with them. Who would have ever imagined that such a small band of socially and politically insignificant people could have turned the world upside down (Acts 17:6)? However, as I study various models of leadership in the church in particular, I find that we have failed to catch the significance of what the Savior has done. Very few pastors spend enough time with their leadership teams to exercise servant-leadership.

I believe that a primary reason for this is today's prevailing cultural model for pastoral ministry. Although we are slow to acknowledge it, our culture plays a bigger role in what pastors do in ministry than we realize. I strongly contend that the cultural model for many of today's pastors, especially in small churches, is based on a rural model where the average pastor spends much of his time visiting his people, along with officiating at weddings and funerals, and preparing some sermons. That is what they expect, and that is usually what they get. The men who make up the boards primarily serve not by shepherding the flock (Acts 20:28; 1 Peter 5: 1, 2) but by meeting once a month to make decisions regarding what is often mundane. Therefore, there is little time left over for servant-leadership that develops leaders who, in turn, shepherd the flock.

However, our times and the culture have changed. The population has shifted from rural to urban America. But people's expectations of what pastors do somehow did not make the transition. The larger urban and suburban churches have forced some change because the senior pastor cannot be expected to visit everyone in the church. Thus, administrative responsibilities have replaced visitation responsibilities in many job descriptions, although some larger churches have hired a minister of visitation. In either case pastors are not spending much time with their board members.

This is the reason why earlier in this book I proposed a new model for pastoral ministry. It is one which I believe includes more of the biblical essentials for ministry. In that model I placed the development of a team of leaders as a top priority for pastors in the church. This is a crucial aspect of servant-leadership which can no longer be neglected if our churches are going to reach the growing number of nonchurched Americans.

Just as important, when pastors or parachurch leaders serve and pour time into their teams, it sends a clear message that they are important and valued by the ministry. Once leaders have gained credibility with their teams, the fact that they take time out of their busy schedules to be with their people, to minister to their spiritual and emotional needs, and to train them for leadership in the church has a way of motivating them for ministry. They, in turn, will repeat the process with others all the way down to the lowliest member. It would be comparable to someone with the stature of a man like Billy Graham taking time to minister to you or me. We would feel honored and challenged to accomplish great things for our Savior as a response to that kind of servant's heart.

Empowerment through Accomplishment

Visionary leaders empower their teams through individual and institutional accomplishment: Team members experience success individually in their separate ministry tasks, and the organization as a whole experiences success in its ministry. As a result, all of those who are a part of the organization feel a sense of accomplishment.

INDIVIDUAL ACCOMPLISHMENT. It is important that team members experience individual accomplishments in a ministry. When this happens, they realize what God can do through them and are motivated to attempt even greater things for God. Thus, wise visionary leaders must seek to involve their people in tasks commensurate with their abilities according to their divine design.

Most good dreams are large, all encompassing, and span a significant period of time. While initially this serves to challenge the ministry community, over the long haul big visions can appear as unattainable. This may overwhelm and bring discouragement in spite of a person's knowledge of his divine design. The solution to this potential problem is for leaders to put on their management hats and exercise their skills in planning. Though more will be said about this area of management in the next chapter, wise planning instructs us to break the dream into accomplishable, "bite-size" tasks.

In *The Leadership Challenge* Kouzes and Posner suggest that the term *planning* fails to convey the emotions that are experienced when someone accomplishes a significant task. They have come up with the more descriptive term *small wins.*[12] Bite size tasks result in small wins, which encourage people and build their commitment to a dream. Therefore, leaders should plan the team's various ministries and break them down in such a way that team members are able to accomplish them with success. Furthermore, as Kouzes and Posner write:

> Small wins build people's confidence levels and reinforce their natural desire to feel successful. Since additional resources generally tend to flow to winners, this means that slightly larger wins can be attempted next. A series of small wins therefore provides a foundation of stable building blocks. Each win preserves gains and makes it harder to return to pre-existing conditions. Like miniature experiments or pilot studies, small wins also provide information that facilitates learning and adaptation."[13]

Nehemiah practiced the strategy of taking bite-size tasks and accomplishing small wins. This is clearly portrayed in

Nehemiah 3 where the work of rebuilding the wall and gates is assigned to various people on the team. It appears that certain individuals were assigned various sections of the wall or gates for repair. One group repaired one of the gates (v. 13), while another group made repairs along the wall (v. 15).

I once implemented a small-wins policy at a church that was in desperate need of renewal. This church, like so many today across America, had been declining in attendance for several years, and some members were even questioning whether they should continue. I was asked to serve as an interim pastor until they located a new person. As I suspected, the church had no ministry vision. Consequently, I began to cast a Great Commission dream for reaching the nonchurched people in the church's community. While the people were excited about the prospect of reaching the nonchurched, how could they accomplish such a task when they were so few in number? The obvious answer was to implement a process of small wins.

To begin, we invited the nonchurched people in the community to hear a "seeker-friendly" sermon from the Scriptures. A seeker-friendly sermon addresses some relevant topic such as discouragement, fear, or anger in such a way that both churched and nonchurched people benefit from the message. A problem was that over the years as attendance declined so had the church's enthusiasm for maintaining the facility where they met. The people, however, had become used to the situation and were blind to the deterioration of the buildings. As a new person at the church, I noticed it immediately, and realized that visitors would also. Facilities in need of repair communicate a loser's image to the community. People naturally question the credibility of any group that would meet under such circumstances.

We set up a small win: repairing and painting the facilities. I preached a positive sermon that explained how cutting-edge churches work hard to maintain the appearance of their facilities. Since this church had caught the vision, they immediately organized a series of work days to repair and improve the facility so that, at the very least, it would be presentable in appearance. The members quickly realized that this goal was bite size and easily attainable. Once they had accomplished this task, they felt good about their work and, even more important, about themselves. The next bite-size task would be even more attainable in light of their accomplishment.

The important lesson here is that not only was the facility improved but so was the congregation's personal esteem. People who had viewed themselves as losers now, through their accomplishment, began to see themselves as winners. This is inevitable when a ministry community experiences a series of wins; in fact, how could they view themselves in any other way?

Of course there will be failures. Many young leaders, whether professional or lay, will not take risks, because they fear failure. They believe that if they fail, then those on the leadership team will lose confidence in their abilities to lead. That is why it is also important to develop an environment where it is permissible to fail. A leader must be willing to fail to succeed. If an environment has not been established where people have freedom to fail, then people will not take risks, and the ministry will either plateau or go into decline.

INSTITUTIONAL ACCOMPLISHMENT. Visionary leaders not only empower their teams through encouraging individual accomplishment, they may do so directly or indirectly through institutional accomplishment as well. In this context I use institutional accomplishment in two ways.

The first is the general success of the church or parachurch ministry as a whole. Successful ministries in themselves empower those on the ministry team. It is hard to argue against success. Small bites and small wins eventually encourage and lead to large bites and large wins. Tired ministry organizations renew themselves and begin to grow again. New ministries start to grow and become larger established churches or parachurch organizations. Ministry tasks that were viewed as much too difficult are now seen as accomplishable. Visionary leaders must be sure to continue the small-wins strategy while pointing to God's obvious blessing of the team's efforts.

I also use institutional accomplishment in the sense of calling people's attention to God's obvious hand of blessing on a ministry. People are empowered when they sense that God is uniquely blessing and honoring their ministry in a way that is not common in other ministries. There is a special sense that God is in this work. Therefore, visionary leaders should be unusually sensitive to these signs and take opportunity to point them out to their ministry teams. In addition, they can regularly remind them of God's blessings and use them when they recast the dream to "rally the troops," especially during any lulls in the ministry.

Nehemiah provides us with an example of this kind of empowerment. In Nehemiah 2:17, 18, he conveys his dream to the Jews who had survived the captivity and were living in reproach in Jerusalem. Immediately prior to his charge to accomplish the dream, he calls their attention to the fact that God has uniquely blessed his efforts thus far (v. 18). He refers to such inspiring events as God's using the pagan King Artaxerxes to allow him to return to Jerusalem and issue letters that would give him access to material with which they could rebuild the gates and wall (2:8). This provides the hope and encouragement they had been waiting for. In spite of their desperate situation, there is little question that God is behind Nehemiah's vision and will bless their efforts to rebuild the wall.

This knowledge of God's special blessing has so affected and empowered Nehemiah that he also refers to it when he faces Israel's enemies. For example, in Nehemiah 2:19 Sanballat and Tobiah mock the Jews and their vision. However, Nehemiah, in the context of his vision message, calls attention to the fact that God will give them success (v. 20). Most likely this is based on God's unique work in the past. I suspect it may have been said within hearing distance of the Jews, although there is no evidence for this in the text.

Empowerment through Delegation

Visionary leaders empower their ministry teams through granting them the power and authority to lead in their areas of ministry influence. There is some debate in leadership circles concerning where the authority to exercise that power rests in an organization. While this is not as much an issue in parachurch ministries, it is in some churches. I refer primarily to churches that are congregational in nature or who exercise elder rule. Without going into great detail, I will say there is often a power struggle between the pastor and the board over who leads and the amount of power and authority behind that leadership. Some churches have adopted a form of lay co-leadership that puts the power in the hands of a lay elder board. In this scheme, often the pastor's leadership role is that he functions as "just another one of the boys." The problem here is that co-leadership results in no leadership. Based on Scripture and experience, I believe the authority scales tip in the favor of the senior pastor who has been trained for leadership as well as preaching and teaching. However, he is to lead not as a tyrant (Matt. 20:25) but as a servant (Mark 10:45).

Assuming that the power to lead and the authority to exercise that power is resident in the ministry organization's primary leader, he in turn will empower his team members by granting them the power and authority necessary to work within their ministry spheres of influence. Again, there has always been a problem in organizations where the person who has power is afraid to delegate that power, rendering those under him practically powerless to accomplish their tasks. In Christian ministry this must not be the case, because God has designed and granted gifts to each believer in the body of Christ for ministry (Rom. 12, 1 Cor. 12, and Eph. 4).

Visionary leaders empower their team members to make the key decisions affecting their particular ministry areas. This means they are free to make key decisions without checking with the primary leader. This also assumes that the leader is training and coaching them so that they have the expertise to make those kinds of decisions. This is esteem-building and communicates confidence in the ministry team. There are several biblical examples of this kind of delegation. In Nehemiah 7:1–3, it appears that Nehemiah delegated his leadership power and authority in this manner. In verse 2 he places Hanani, his brother, and Hananiah, his military commander, in charge of Jerusalem. However, along with this delegation, he gives them some coaching (v. 3). In Exodus 18, Jethro, Moses' father-in-law, observes how much of Moses' time is spent in settling the disputes of the people of Israel. He then provides Moses with some excellent advice, for he points out the need to delegate much of this responsibility to other competent, qualified people (18:17–23). Moses gives these men the power and authority to settle all minor disputes while he handles the major disputes (18:26).

Empowerment through Modeling

Visionary leaders empower their teams through their own examples of sustained excellence. Leaders themselves are examples of what the ministry organization is all about. To understand a ministry and its mission, observe the leader, which is exactly what people on the ministry team do.

This comes as no surprise to those in Christian leadership, because repeatedly Scripture emphasizes the importance of personal example for others. On numerous occasions Paul exhorts his followers not only to observe his example but also to follow his example: 1 Corinthians 4:14–17, 11:1; Philippians 3:17, 4:9; and 1 Thessalonians 1:6. In 2 Thessalonians 3:8, 9, Paul states that he paid for his own food and worked to meet his own support needs to be a model and an example to the believers in the church at Thessalonica. Whether their lives are good or bad, leaders are models to their followers. Paul's desire was to provide a model of sustained excellence that would attract disciples and bring glory to his Savior. In particular, modeling empowers a team in several important ways.

CREDIBILITY AND EMULATION. Leaders whose lives are consistent with what they profess both gain credibility and encourage their followers to emulate their behavior. Although leaders have the authority to exercise power, it is their behavior not their position that brings them the respect and credibility. Paul acknowledges this truth in 1 Corinthians 9:1–14 where he alludes to his rights as an apostle but states that he has chosen not to exercise these rights because of some potential negative impact on his leadership and the preaching of the gospel (vv. 15–19).

That same behavior, in turn, not only gains leaders credibility but gives incentive for others to behave in a similar fashion and become models in their own right. Paul describes this in 1 Thessalonians 1:5, 6:

> For our gospel did not come to you in word only, but also in power and in the Holy Spirit and with full conviction; just as you know what kind of men we proved to be among you for your sake. You also became imitators of us and of the Lord, having received the word in much tribulation with the joy of the Holy Spirit, so that you became an example to all the believers in Macedonia and in Achaia.

VALUES. Personal examples empower followers by imparting to them what leaders value, the things most important to them, which penetrate to the very depths of their beings and give meaning to their lives. Values affect every area of life and belief and exert a profound influence on co-workers. Kouzes and Posner cite research that shows effective companies communicate their values through clarity, consensus, and intensity.[14]

Good visionary leaders incarnate their values clearly by preaching and living them to such an extent that those who make up the ministry team are able to articulate them.

Good visionary leaders live and communicate their values in such a way that not only do their teams know what they are, but are committed to them. This is ministry consensus. It is prevalent in parachurch ministries because their values are extremely focused and so pronounced. Indeed, they are known in the Christian community for those particular values, and the ministry team is recruited because of an affinity for them. Supporters select and contribute to these ministries because of a commitment to these same values. The typical American evangelical church has a strong set of values most often expressed in a doctrinal statement. In churches that subscribe to a membership, agreement with the doctrinal statement is essential. The ministry team is recruited on the basis of their commitment to these values, and most on the ministry team, if you should ask, would consider dying for them.

Good visionary leaders feel very strongly about certain values. They are held with intensity. It is not that they merely agree with certain values, but those values are esteemed and practiced almost daily. People do not have to be reminded periodically of these values, for they are ingrained in everything the leader does. Again, this is the heart of the parachurch movement. Most parachurch organizations hold certain biblical values with intensity. Most likely, the founder of the organization was deeply affected by those values, and his or her life has mirrored them consistently in their public and private ministries. If a parachurch ministry begins to plateau or decline, it is often because the founder dies and is replaced by someone who holds the same values with less intensity, or because the organization has not developed more culturally relevant ways of implementing those values in the ministry.

I believe that one of the differences between the 85 percent of American churches that are either stagnant or dying and the 15 percent that are not is the intensity to which they hold to their values whatever they may be. I suspect that all of those which are evangelical, and there are many in that 85 percent, have strong doctrinal statements. If you were to ask them what they believe, they could quickly and vigorously produce a doctrinal statement. And the members of those churches agree with that doctrinal statement. While they have clarity and consensus on their values, they come up short on intensity. If on a Sunday morning you were to step into the pulpit and ask how many people believe evangelism is important, all would raise their hands. That reflects clarity and consensus. However, if you were to ask how many people had presented the gospel of Christ to some other person within the last few months, very few hands would go up. That reflects a lack of intensity.

Those evangelical churches that are growing as a result of conversion growth most often are led by people who value the Great Commission with intensity. They do not simply talk about evangelism and discipleship, they vigorously evangelize people using culturally relevant and effective methods. Evangelism and discipleship are major topics of discussion and are highly esteemed among those on the ministry team. When they tell stories, they usually are about how someone came to faith or is growing in and proclaiming the faith. Even among the members are intense feelings about seeing people come to faith who are followed up through a program of aggressive discipleship. However, the important thing to remember in all this is that their feelings reflect those of the pastor of the church. They look to him as the mission point person to model how they should behave.

Encouraging the Team

The fifth step in building the team is to encourage the members.

I suspect that there is some overlap between empowering a team and encouraging a team. Both help a team overcome the various obstacles they are sure to meet as they move toward the vision.

However, as I use the terms, they approach the obstacle from two different angles. On one hand, empowerment prepares the team and each of its members to encounter and overcome various obstacles. On the other hand, encouragement helps the team and any of its people who have been snagged and held up by the obstacle to break free. Encouragement "jump starts" a ministry whose battery is run down or provides a sudden burst of energy to help it through a difficult time. No matter how empowered a group may be, if it faces enough obstacles, the ministry will slow down. Encouragement reaches out a helping hand to those on the team who are discouraged and have dropped out or are contemplating the same (Acts 14:21, 22).

The Problem of Discouragement

I have discovered over the years as a church pastor and as one in a seminary who prepares men and women for ministry that discouragement is a major obstacle (if not *the* major obstacle) to ministry and the accomplishment of a dream. Just recently I read a letter from a young man in pastoral ministry in the Midwest. The letter was addressed to his friends letting them know that he was dropping out of the ministry for a while to recuperate from the discouragement and depression he had experienced as the result of attempting to plant a church. He had decided to start a church but without adequate preparation. As he and his small team attempted to move down the field, they encountered waves of obstacles that took a heavy toll. Discouragement set in, quickly followed by depression, which led to the pastor's eventual resignation from the team. As I read the letter I caught in his words such an overwhelming sense of failure that I question if he will ever return to professional pastoral ministry.

We must also keep in mind that it can happen to the best of us. No one is exempt. For example, one of the most discouraging portions of Scripture is 2 Timothy 4:9–16. The entire section, which was written toward the end of Paul's life, "drips" with discouragement. Why was he so discouraged? First, many of his friends had deserted him at a time when he needed their support (vv. 10, 16). Second, his enemies, in particular Alexander who was a coppersmith, had attacked him

(vv. 14, 15). Finally, except for Luke's company, he was all alone in a Roman dungeon (v. 11). Perhaps he sensed that the end was near (v. 6) because, according to tradition, he was beheaded soon after this event. Discouragement attacks anyone regardless of race, creed, or religion. It is no respecter of persons. It does not care if you are one of Christ's apostles, the leader of a team, or a team member.

The Solution of Encouragement

The obvious solution to the obstacle of discouragement is encouragement. Visionary leaders must spend time encouraging their ministry teams. It provides them with hope that helps them to break free from the web of obstacles that hinder or momentarily slow them down.

I believe that one of the keys to the success of Paul's early ministry was his teammate Barnabas. God's distinctive mark on Barnabas' life was his ability to encourage. In fact, though his name was Joseph, according to Acts 4:36, he was called Barnabas by the apostles, which means son of encouragement. We get a glimpse of why in Acts 11:22, 23 when the church at Jerusalem sent him to Antioch where he encouraged the believers to remain true to the Lord.

But how might a leader encourage people on a regular basis? What can he do to assign it its proper place in his team-crafting efforts? Interestingly, not much has been written in leadership material on encouragement. However, Kouzes and Posner have recognized the importance of encouragement to leadership and in *The Leadership Challenge* have assigned it a major section (two chapters) entitled "Encouraging the Heart." They suggest that leaders encourage their people in two ways: by recognizing individual achievements and by celebrating the efforts of the entire group.[15] Both methods are reflected in the Scriptures.

RECOGNIZE INDIVIDUAL ACHIEVEMENTS. Visionary leaders encourage their teams by recognizing their people and their individual ministry accomplishments. This is because God values people and what they do for his glory. In spite of the fall, people are still valuable and important to God. He created them in his image (Gen. 1:26, 27). In Matthew 6:26, the Savior indicates that human life is worth far more than animal life. Then, in Mark 8:36, 37, Jesus asserts that a man's soul is far more valuable than the wealth and possessions of the entire world. God also values man's work when it is done for him (Eph. 6:5–8; Col. 3:22–25).

However, visionary leaders should expect the best from themselves and their team members. Kouzes and Posner state that "successful leaders have high expectations, both of themselves and of their followers."[16] I find that often this is not the case in many ministry organizations, especially the church. Far too many settle for mediocrity in ministry. Perhaps this is because so many churches are small and viewed as extended families; consequently, the family does not mind as much if a member who is a Sunday school teacher is "winging it." The important thing is that the kids have a teacher, and the fact that the individual cannot teach is something to deal with later. While members do not notice it, today's nonchurched visitors who are used to excellence do notice it.

To the contrary, Scripture encourages the pursuit of excellence. Excellence was important in the Old Testament. Worship was characterized by excellence. The Jews were to offer only their best animals as sacrifices to God in their worship (Lev. 22:20, 22). Excellence was important as well in the New Testament. A man's work was to be accomplished "as to the Lord, and not to men" (Eph. 6:7; Col. 3:23). Excellence also characterizes God and what he does. In fact, he gave his very best when he gave us his Son, Jesus Christ.

Not only does God value people's best accomplishments for him, he rewards those works. Scripture has much to say about rewards (1 Cor. 3:8, 10–15; 4:5; 9:17). In the future, at the judgment seat of Christ (2 Cor. 5:10), God will reward the Christian's works (1 Cor. 3:10–15). It is important to note that the basis for this reward is said to be "the quality of each man's work" (1 Cor. 3:13). If God values people and their good works of service for him, then it makes sense that we do the same. As a pastor in one church, I did not believe in publicly acknowledging people for God's accomplishments through their lives. My reasoning was that I was afraid I might leave someone out and offend him. Of course, this is always a danger, but the opposite extreme of not giving due recognition, in my opinion, is far worse.

In fact, leaders must seek to avoid two extremes. One extreme errs by failing to recognize any of the accomplishments of their people. This sends a clear message that who they are and what they do is not important. The result, however, is that people stop caring and the ministry begins to die. The other extreme errs by attempting to recognize everything a person does. The problem here is that after a while the recognition loses its value and is taken for granted. Leaders should seek to acknowledge the legitimate accomplishments of their people in some beneficial way that moves the ministry toward the accomplishment of its dream.

Both the church and the parachurch organizations can recognize people in two ways. First, they can set up a formal system of awards. This includes such things as bonuses, raises, award ceremonies, and promotions where possible. Some ministry organizations do not practice this because they feel it is a gimmick developed by the secular world that is not necessary in God's work. This is a grave mistake, because formal awards announce to those on the team that their good accomplishments for the Savior are valued. However, the problem with a formal award system is that people begin to expect them and eventually may not see them as rewards but as a part of their ministry compensation.

The second way is to reward people informally. This can take place either in public or private. It includes lots of intangible rewards such as personal recognition through verbal and written praise, thank-you notes, being personally available to them, and so on. These methods are used repeatedly in the Scriptures. For example, Paul gives public thanks for various churches in his writings and recognizes their works for the Savior (Col. 1:3, 4; 1 Thess. 1:2–10). He also singles out individuals and commends them to others based on what God has done through them. He did this with Timothy (Phil. 2:20, 22), Epaphroditus (Phil. 2:29, 30), and Judas and Silas (Acts 15:25–27). I do not believe this was mere flattery or an attempt on his part to win a hearing, because on other occasions he would not praise but would confront problem churches such as in Galatia (Gal. 1:1–10) and people who were in error such as Peter (Gal. 2:11–14).

CELEBRATE TEAM ACCOMPLISHMENTS. Not only can leaders encourage their team members individually, they can encourage the team as a whole. Kouzes and Posner suggest that one way to do this well is through both cheerleading and public celebration.[17]

In a very important sense, the primary leaders of ministries should be cheerleaders. Every ministry needs its cheerleaders to encourage people to work together during the tough times as well as the good times. What happens in a football game when the home team is on defense and the opposition has the ball on their one-foot line? The cheerleaders go to work, and we hear, "Push 'em back, push 'em back, way back!" The world of athletics has discovered the strength of team loyalty, why not the parachurch and the church?

It is also interesting to note that in athletics, victories are often followed by celebrations. Athletes and fans are quick to celebrate their accomplishments. Why are Christian organizations often reluctant to do the same? They did so in the Old Testament. For example, Nehemiah led the Jews in Jerusalem in rebuilding the wall and gates of the city. This accomplished their vision. However, there was more to come: a dedication of the walls with a public celebration of worship to God acknowledging what he had done through the people (Neh. 12:27–47). This was a time of great celebrative worship involving two choirs, a band, singing, and the offering of sacrifices.

But what do visionary leaders celebrate? A celebration by nature has an object; something is being celebrated. Thus, it makes sense to celebrate the things that are important to the ministry organization. Certainly, the accomplishment of a vision is a major cause for celebration, as mirrored by the events of Nehemiah 12. Also, the accomplishment of various ministry goals that lead to the vision or the removal of obstacles that could hinder it are causes for celebration. Some ministry organizations celebrate important events. For example, schools have graduations and founders' day banquets. Churches celebrate the purchase or completion of new facilities, the accomplishment of a critical growth goal, or the addition of new staff. Some create special events for the purpose of celebration, such as a Celebration of Friendship Sunday. These celebrations also provide good opportunities for enhancing team relationships, the communication of ideas, good fellowship, and stress relief.

8

Wearing the Management Hat

Developing a Ministry Plan

Not only was Pastor Bob excited, his team was, too. Most of them had suited up and were moving down the gridiron together with an eye toward putting the ball in the end zone. What had happened? Why the change?

Pastor Bob had implemented some key team building concepts. An example was the last board retreat. He did a series of four short messages on the doctrine of God's grace in the Christian's life. Then he told how in his personal experiences this knowledge had revolutionized his perspective on life in terms of his self-worth. The men listened intently. They understood salvation by grace through faith in Christ but had not thought a lot about grace and its place in the Christian life. Most did not realize that because of God's grace in Christ they did not have to meet certain standards or be accepted by others to feel significant. They wanted to know more. What began as a one-hour session lasted into the early hours of the morning.

In the ensuing weeks, several wives called and asked Pastor Bob what had happened at the retreat. Their husbands seemed different, and they liked the difference. One wife said that her husband came home one evening and apologized for being a workaholic. Since then he had spent less time with his business and more time with his family.

Also, Pastor Bob began to spend more of his time with each man individually as their busy schedules permitted. They would either meet for breakfast or lunch. Whereas previously they met mostly for Bible study and prayer, Bob began to help them discover who they were in terms of their divine design. They discovered their gifts, passions, leadership styles, and temperaments. Thus they began to develop a personal strategy for individual ministry. Eventually most of the board became involved in some type of personal ministry either within or outside the church.

They began to view the church as a base for ministry as well as a place for ministry. This made some people angry, because several board members announced they would resign their teaching positions at the end of the year. They felt they were in the wrong place; they described themselves as "round pegs in square holes." Of course, Brother Bill, as the Sunday school superintendent, was among the unhappy ones.

Not much had changed with Brother Bill. As far as the vision was concerned, his uniform was still hanging in his locker. He became the lone voice of constant dissent on the board. While most of those on the board were unhappy about the time he took up in their meetings, God used the opportunity to teach them patience and good listening skills.

The church had begun to grow in response to many of the new changes. Some people had caught the vision for reaching their nonchurched friends and felt comfortable about bringing them to the contemporary worship service at 9:30 A.M. or to one of the seeker-oriented Bible studies in the homes of some of the couples in the church.

What increasingly became a major problem for Pastor Bob was that the growth of the church had increased the complexity of the church. He learned that to accomplish his dream for this church, he would have to become comfortable wearing two hats, one of leadership and the other of management. He could hire another staff person to help, but he desperately needed a worship leader. While most of his preparation in business and seminary had been in management, he felt his gifts lay more in the area of leadership, evidenced by his abilities to build his team and lead the church to new growth. Consequently, he had learned to work hard in both leadership and management.

As stated in chapter 6, leadership and management are two separate but complementary functions, and both are essential if any ministry is to survive in the twenty-first century. One without the other can spell disaster. But what is the difference, and how can a visionary leader both lead and manage a ministry effectively in the twenty-first century? In chapter 6, I introduced some of these concepts but with an emphasis on leadership. However, in this chapter, the focus is more on management. I will briefly address the basic differences between management and leadership and then spend the rest of the chapter on how to develop a ministry plan.

Distinguishing Management from Leadership

Key to effective ministry in any Christian organization is an understanding of the foundational distinction between management and leadership. Both are necessary and yet both are different in their roles and what they accomplish. To understand this, first we will look briefly at the background of modern management. Then we will examine and explain the differences between management and leadership.

The Background

A knowledge of the recent development of modern day management in relation to leadership can be helpful in understanding the difference between the two. In *A Force for Change* John Kotter gives us some helpful background information which summarizes this development:

> Leadership is an ageless topic. That which we call management is largely the product of the last 100 years, a

response to one of the most significant developments of the twentieth century: the emergence of large numbers of complex organizations. Modern management was invented, in a sense, to help the new railroads, steel mills, and auto companies achieve what legendary entrepreneurs created them for. Without such management, these complex enterprises tended to become chaotic in ways that threatened their very existence. Good management brought a degree of order and consistency to key dimensions like the quality and profitability of products.[1]

The problem for many secular and ministry organizations is that this relatively recent emphasis on management has blurred the distinction between the two, with the result that many have mistakenly replaced leadership with management. Therefore, leadership has become management. Consequently, many of these organizations are run by managers, not leaders.

Over time, the results of management without leadership have had an adverse effect on ministry organizations. Many church and parachurch ministries have become inflexible and have not adapted to the important changes taking place around them, with the result that many are in trouble. For example, Leith Anderson in *Dying for Change* writes of the church that "an estimated 85 percent of America's Protestant churches are either stagnating or dying."[2] Increasingly, the parachurch is facing the same. A few lines down, he adds, "Parallel to the churches of America are a large number of parachurch organizations that were born and blossomed with the post-World War II 'baby boom.'"[3]

This does not mean that management and managers are bad. Nor does it mean that we should get rid of management and replace it with leadership. It demonstrates the results of one without the other. Management does not cope well with change. But leadership without management is equally devastating, because leadership does not cope well with the complexity that change produces.

190

The Distinction

The basic difference between leadership and management is that the former strives to accomplish change, while the latter seeks to control complexity.[4] I said this in an earlier chapter, but what does this mean? Our world is changing at a phenomenal rate. For example, George Barna writes: "Whether or not each of the predictions about the future contained in this book come true, one thing is certain: America will be substantially different in the year 2000. Unparalleled change will sweep the nation, and transform every dimension of life in this country."[5] Then he explains what this means for Christian ministry organizations and the body of Christ in the following:

> Clearly, the Christian Body cannot hope to have much of an impact if we respond in the same ways we have in the past. These are new challenges, demanding creative, unique responses. The solutions that worked ten or even five years ago will fail in the coming decade. We are being confronted with a new wave of obstacles and opportunities. After careful study of our options, and discerning the mind of God, we must tailor new strategies to address this new environment.[6]

This is what leadership clearly is all about. It seeks to help the ministry organization not only survive but thrive by coping with this tremendous change. The way it accomplishes this is different from management. First, leadership develops a profound, positive vision for the ministry organization's future along with strategies for coping with and producing the useful changes needed to achieve the vision. Next, it communicates that vision to all who are in a position to influence its realization. Finally, it builds a team of leaders who own and are empowered by that vision to accomplish the same. These aspects of leadership have been covered thus far and make up the thrust of this book.

At this point many people err regarding the relationship of management with leadership. Though some understand that there is a distinction, they believe that management is the implementation part of leadership. But this is not the case. Leadership, as seen above, has its own implementation process. Obviously leadership in attempting to cope with the tremendous change taking place in this world must also produce useful change in the church. However, the result of this change in the church is increasing complexity and chaos for the ministry. And the greater the change in the church, the greater the complexity.

Management concerns complexity. It is the function of management to help the ministry organization control this complexity in the church, with the result that the ministry thrives in the midst of its own chaos and complexity.[7]

The way management accomplishes this is different from leadership. First, management does the planning and budgeting. It sets goals and establishes steps to accomplish these goals, including a timetable and the allocation of necessary resources. Next, it sets up an organizational structure and flexible job descriptions within that structure, employing staff who best fit those job descriptions and delegating to them the responsibility for carrying out the plan. Finally, it monitors the results and solves any problems that surface in implementing the plan.

I should also mention at this point that Scripture distinguishes between management and leadership in terms of spiritual gifts.[8] In Romans 12:8, Paul includes leadership as one of the gifts from God to be exercised as a part of the body of Christ. Also, in 1 Corinthians 12:28, he identifies the gift of administration, which is essentially the same as management. While to some degree there are people in ministry organizations who lead and manage, there are others, according to Paul, who are spiritually gifted in these areas to accomplish the ministry's dream. I believe that not only do some Christians have one gift and some the other, but there are Christians who have the decided advantage of possessing both gifts. This would mean that such an individual with training and experience would have extraordinary abilities to both lead and manage a ministry and accomplish much for the Savior. In addition, this is why an excellent gifts assessment program is so important to any ministry organization.

Now that I have reviewed the foundational difference between leadership and management, the rest of the chapter will focus on management. The idea here is to help visionary leaders like Pastor Bob develop a ministry plan. However, this must not be just another plan. The problem with plans is that far too often they are boring things that have the potential to stifle, not kindle the flame of a good vision. The purpose of the rest of this chapter is to present the benefits of planning and to aid visionary leaders in developing visually attractive, marketable ministry plans that have the power to motivate both them and other people so that they thrive on chaos and complexity in the midst of an exciting ministry.

The Benefits of a Ministry Plan

Why develop a ministry plan? Is it simply a management perk or is it really necessary? What practical value does it provide for visionary organizations that are led by promising visionary leaders? While there are several benefits, this section will briefly outline four: the reality check, the determination of the future, the planning document, and ministry credibility.

A Reality Check

One benefit of a plan is that it complements the vision by being a useful reality check on the vision.[9] It answers numerous questions such as, Is this vision in touch with reality? How will we fund this vision? Do we have sufficient leaders to accomplish the vision? If not, where will we find them? In short, the plan serves as a necessary bridge between the abstract world of dreaming and the concrete world of reality. Often the plan, like a searing summer morning sun, will cause the dreams of the night to evaporate quickly.

An example of this kind of reality check is found in the leadership of Nehemiah. A key part of his plan was to petition King Artaxerxes to allow him to return to Jerusalem and to rebuild the wall and gates. This was an unbelievably bold request in light of the fact that earlier, when the people were rebuilding the walls (Ezra 4:12), Artaxerxes was the very one who had issued a decree that they stop (Ezra 4:19–23). Nehemiah asked the king to reverse that decree, and it could have cost him his life. This would have seemed like an impossible task to an ordinary man, but not Nehemiah. Of course, the king granted his request (Neh. 2:8), which not only enhanced the plan and its progress but served as a reality check on the vision that the Jews in Jerusalem would be spiritually renewed and glorify, again, their great God.

The Determination of the Future

Few people in this world would not like to have some say about their future. The point here is that we can. Another benefit in developing a ministry plan is that the participants have a part in determining their future.

Some people take a reactive, passive posture in life in general and the future in particular. They view the future with the attitude that "whatever will be, will be." They make up life's observers and reactors. Consequently, they bounce through life responding to its bumps much like the ball in a pinball machine. In these situations life sits in the driver's seat and dictates their future. After hearing about the dreadful situation in Jerusalem, Nehemiah could have relaxed and waited for God to do something. If God was really behind this vision, then perhaps Artaxerxes would first come to him and suggest that he go to Jerusalem and rebuild the wall and gates. Maybe the Jews who had escaped the captivity would take the initiative and send an envoy to Nehemiah asking him to come cast his vision and then lead them in the accomplishment of the same. Either way, by waiting on God, Nehemiah could have been sure that he was in it.

Other people prefer a proactive over a reactive response to life. Rather than allow life and its daily circumstances to dictate their future, they take control and to a certain degree determine their own future. They, in turn, sit in the driver's seat and are seldom caught by surprises. They accomplish this through careful, creative planning. Nehemiah did not wait for some sign or miraculous movement of God. Rather than wait for God to move him, he realized that God was waiting for him to move, and, thus, he took the initiative.

We must realize that our God is an initiator. He took the initiative and created the world and mankind. When the entire human race fell, through Adam, God took the initiative and sent the Savior into the world to die for the world. And it is most important to realize that this took place according to a predetermined plan (Acts 2:22, 23). He also gave us the Great Commission vision and instructed us to go (Matt. 28:19; Mark 16:15) and not wait for people to come to us.

The Planning Document

A third benefit in developing a ministry plan is that it places in the hands of the people an attractive, motivational planning document. This visually communicates the goals and objectives of the plan and the part they play in the process of getting there. No one person can accomplish the ministry plan. It takes people, often lots of people, to realize the plan. Planning establishes ministry goals, the specific steps to take, and the necessary finances to achieve these goals as well as other things. But planning also involves people. The important component, if not the most important component, in any plan concerns the people or ministry community who are to be a part of that plan. It is essential that the ministry community not only know the plan but how they fit into the plan. This can be accomplished by placing a copy of a well-designed, inspiring ministry plan in their hands for perusal at their convenience.

Ministry Credibility

A fourth benefit in establishing a ministry plan is that it brings credibility to the ministry organization. A clear, comprehensive plan sends a message to the Christian and non-Christian community and its constituency that this ministry is not "winging it." A lot of significant, careful thought has gone into the development of this ministry organization. Its leaders have done their homework. They know exactly who they are in their design and ministry capabilities. They know precisely where they are going, because they have developed and articulated a credible vision and a strategy to accomplish the same. Finally, they are not so idealistic that they have not considered the critical area of finances. The result is believability, which brings respect and admiration and, hopefully, personal commitment.

A carefully developed plan can be especially important to church and parachurch planting ministries. Those who would lead these ministries must realize the importance of establishing credibility. These ministries by nature are new and unproven. The tendency on the part of many people is to stand back and watch to see if they survive. However, this is the exact opposite of what the leaders want. Instead, they need to attract these people to some kind of involvement in the ministry. One important way to accomplish this is through a highly believable plan.

A major obstacle for church and parachurch planting ministries is attracting potential people and initial funding for the project. These ministries cannot begin and survive without people. Both will need personnel and, in the case of church planting, a sizable core group of people. Actually, some studies indicate that the core group needs to consist of fifty or more people if it is to survive and grow into a larger church.

In addition, these ministries for the most part cannot begin and survive without finances. Funding is necessary to cover such start-up expenses as salaries, facilities, advertising, and other needs. Ministry credibility is essential to the obtaining of funds. The risk is far too great for people to invest their money and, even more costly, their time in a ministry that projects questionable believability. An "up front package" consisting of a positive, compelling vision of the future and its strategy complemented by a coherent, attractive plan wins high believability.

Factors Affecting a Ministry Plan

How do you actually develop a plan? What factors should be considered? At least four factors in the development of a coherent, attractive ministry plan are the time frame, process, contents, and visual appearance of the plan.

The Time Frame

Whereas the vision by nature covers a longer time frame of several years, plans must focus on time frames ranging from a few months to a few years. The reason is that tremendous change continues to create a dynamic environment. The unexpected is now to be expected. Yet when the unexpected happens, most often plans have to be altered or tossed and new plans designed. In fact, Kotter states that some businesses, "consider 'long-term planning' an oxymoron."[10] Consequently, while detailed planning is, indeed, important in our dynamic culture, it should be short-term and not long-term. Anything else may prove to be a waste of people's time and energy and ultimately discourage future planning activities.

The Process

The visionary leader and his planning team will need to work through the following three steps of the planning process. First is to determine and then write down the ministry goals. This answers the important question, What exactly are we trying to accomplish? It includes action steps which should be accompanied by a brief explanation. Second is to design a calendar of events. This answers the question, Approximately when will this take place? It considers the time frame of the plan and its ministry goals and seeks to determine their dates. Third is to establish a budget. This answers the question, How much will this cost us? It focuses attention on the resources needed to accomplish the ministry goals within their allotted time frames.

The Contents

The contents of the printed ministry plan include the goals, calendar of events, budget, and other pertinent information.

It is important to remember that the contents of most plans are boring things which often encourage insomnia rather than prevent it. This does not have to be. Instead, if the plan is well designed in its language and graphics, it can motivate people toward its implementation.

I have included, as an example, a plan designed by Mark Allen for planting Midlothian Community Church in the Brandermill community of Richmond, Virginia.[11] I will refer to this plan throughout the rest of this section and encourage the reader to do the same for maximum comprehension. The contents of the plan should include in order several items.

First in the contents of the plan is a statement of need, which consists of a general explanation of the desire to start a new ministry or of where to take an existing ministry. In church planting, people instinctively ask, "Why would anyone want to start a new church in this community? Don't we have enough churches already?" This is especially true in the South. The need statement should answer this question in such a way that people will read further. The need statement for Midlothian Community Church is:

A culturally relevant church that enables believers to reach the unchurched community of Midlothian, a suburb of Richmond, VA.

It is broad in that the focus is the need in the community for a Great Commission church. However, at the same time it specifies that there is a need for a church that is in touch with and relevant to its culture. It also sees a need to use believers

198

to reach a specific group, the unchurched. The statement has the potential to attract people to the new work.

The need statement may include other information such as current, national, and local trends gained as the result of demographic and psychographic studies. The reason for including them is that they lend statistical support to the idea that there is, indeed, a special need for this kind of church in the community. While most people do not understand statistical information, they do give it high marks for credibility. Note that the Midlothian need statement focuses on baby boomers and then narrows that focus to the particular community as it seeks to demonstrate need.

Second in the contents of the plan is the vision, which supplies the best solution to the need that has previously been articulated. Start with the vision slogan, not the vision statement. A well-designed slogan will attract attention and either communicate the vision or invite people to read further. Next, the slogan should be followed with a concise vision statement of not more than a couple of paragraphs. This provides additional information in case people are not able to catch the vision from the slogan alone or are curious and want more information.

The Midlothian slogan is:

Building a community to serve a community.

This slogan is short and catches the eye. Also, it repeats a popular, relevant term, *community*, which is growing in use in many contemporary churches in America as well as among nonchurched people who are becoming more community conscious.

Third in the contents of the plan is the strategy, which explains how the ministry will implement the vision. The Midlothian strategy statement has five parts. Each carefully and cleverly borrows the term *community* from the vision statement and expands on it in each of the strategies, using it in a slightly different way. For example, there are a core community, an open community, a new community, community groups, and community service. None are the same, but all are tied together in the same package by the same term, which also relates all five back to the vision slogan.

The Midlothian strategy statement is followed by two additional pages that provide further strategy clarification. The first is a definition of terms to make sure the reader understands the various uses of *community*. The second provides a graphic, which explains visually in stair-step fashion how the strategy unfolds.

Fourth in the contents of the plan is the statement of goals. Technically, this is where the planning stage, which is a function of management, actually begins in the document. Both the vision and the strategy, which are functions of leadership, precede this stage and focus it so that it can be realistically carried out.

Note the shift here from the abstract realm of vision and strategy to the concrete, practical realm of planning and budgets. At the same time, the plan serves as a practical reality check on the vision. For example, in the Midlothian document, the strategy was arrived at inductively and involved the abstract idea of developing a core group. The goal was arrived at deductively from the strategy and involved the practical steps of identifying, recruiting, and training twenty members of a core community.

Fifth in the contents of the plan is the calendar of events. The visionary planner will determine when each goal is to be accomplished. Again, contrary to the vision statement, the time frame is much smaller. The Midlothian document sets up a calendar based on ten months. A key is located in the upper left-hand corner of the document to explain the various notations on the calendar itself.

Sixth in the contents of the plan is the budget: funds that will be needed and the sources of those funds. Church and parachurch planting will necessitate both personal and ministry expenses. Established works usually list ministry expenses, and any personal expenses are included under salaries. The former is reflected in the Midlothian document.

The Appearance

The appearance of the planning document is more important than most realize. It has a subtle influence affecting how people will respond to the plan. When the document is attractive and well designed, it casts a shadow of high credibility and integrity on the ministry in general and the plan in particular. When it is poorly designed and not especially attractive, the opposite occurs. I would suggest that most visionary leaders seek professional help as in the case of the Midlothian document, which used Thompson Design in Mesquite, Texas. Another option here is to find a professionally designed document you favor and use it as a guide to plan your own unique design. It is also important to remember that the document must be designed with the people in mind who are going to receive and read the document.

The Midlothian document has several features which enhance the design and integrity of any document. First, there is a lot of white space. This is very pleasing to the eye and attracts the reader's attention. It shows that this document will not be a chore to read, whereas, documents that fill up the page with print have the opposite effect. Second, the font looks contemporary and popular and would appear attractive to baby boomers, who are the document's target audience. Third, there are small, unobtrusive pictures in the margins to illustrate the information on the page. Fourth, the document has footnotes with additional information. This same kind of information could also have a nice effect in the document if it were included in the same place on the page but not necessarily as a footnote.

There remains at least one more step in the envisioning process. It is the preservation of the vision. This important step is taken up in the last chapter.

Midlothian Community Church

Ten-Month Strategic Plan
9/90—6/91

(Preliminary Version)

Need:

A culturally relevant church that enables believers to reach the unchurched community of Midlothian, a suburb of Richmond, Virginia.

Baby Boomers:

- 53 million baby boomers are estimated to be un-churched.[1]
- The average baby boomer attends church only 6.2 times a year—fewer than half as often as those over 40.[2]

Richmond:

- Only one Dallas Seminary graduate serves in the Richmond metropolitan area [population 550,000].[3]

Chesterfield County:

- In the past several years, Chesterfield County has been one of the fastest growing counties in the U.S.[4]
- Eight thousand people are projected to move into Chesterfield County in the next year.[5]

Midlothian:

- Two thousand people are projected to move into Midlothian in the next year.[6]

Brandermill Community:

[the initial site for the church plant]

- Eighty percent of Brandermill's residents are un-churched.[7]
- Eighty-nine percent are business persons and profes-sionals.[8]
- Fifty percent have moved to Brandermill from out of town.[9]
- The average age is thirty-four.[10]

Vision:

Building a Community to Serve a Community

The vision is a culturally relevant church with a Great Commission vision, which empowers people to communicate Christ through significant relationships* with God, other believers, and nonbelievers. The dream is to raise up a community church which reaches out to an unchurched community.

* According to church growth expert Win Arn, 70 to 80 percent of those attracted to church come because they have been invited through a relationship with a friend or relative.

Strategy:

Develop a community of believers prepared to reach a community of nonbelievers:

(1) through **developing a Core Community** [from Sept. 5 to Jan. 6]
   - from whom the leadership community of three couples/singles will be formed [on Jan. 10]
   - by whom the technigrowth campaign will be executed [beginning Jan. 14]

(2) through **providing an Open Community** to which unchurched seekers will be invited through the core community's personal relationships and technigrowth contacts [beginning Mar. 31]

(3) through **providing a New Community** to which believers will be invited for contemporary worship, relevant exposition, and vision sharing [beginning May 1]

(4) through **forming three Community Groups** for believers who desire to encourage one another in their relationship with God, other believers, and nonchurched friends [beginning June 6]
   - who will consist of members of the original core community and the new community
   - who will be led by the 3 couples/singles of the leadership community

(5) through **developing Community Service** in which believers in community groups creatively reach out to serve the Midlothian community [first development after the ten month strategic plan]

Summary of Strategy:

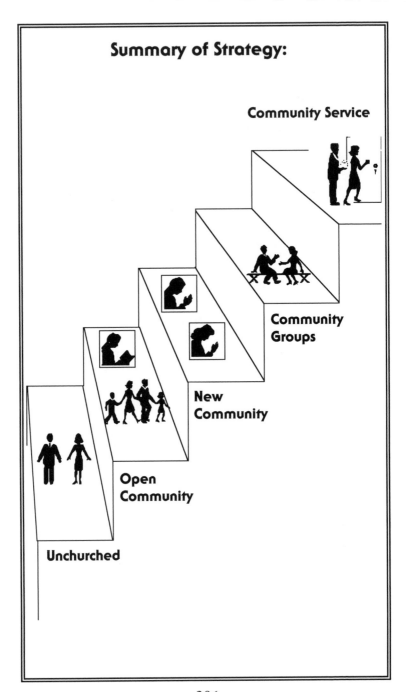

Community Service

Community Groups

New Community

Open Community

Unchurched

206

Definitions:

Core Community: A group of believers living in the targeted community who provide the initial physical and spiritual resources to plant the church.

Leadership Community: A leadership team selected from the original core community and consisting of the leaders of the community groups.

Open Community: A service designed for people who are investigating Christianity as well as those interested in learning how to apply biblical principles to everyday life.

New Community: A service designed for believers interested in deepening their relationship with God through contemporary worship and relevant biblical exposition.

Community Groups: Small groups of 12–13 people designed to enhance a believer's growth in his relationship with God, other believers, and unchurched friends.

Community Service: A creative outreach, developed in community groups, to serve the Midlothian community.

Goals:

(1) **Identify/Recruit/Train 20 members of a Core Community** [Core Group]
Characteristics of this group:
- must be willing to participate in and share in the vision
- must make a long-term commitment.
- should commit to some type of financial support
- should participate in a technigrowth program.
- should serve in and during the open community
- should assimilate into the new community and community groups

(2) **Identify/Train three couples/singles for the Leadership Community**
[Small Group Leaders]
Characteristics of this group:
- must be members of the core community
- must possess leadership abilities in transferring and modeling the vision
- must commit to leading a community group

(3) **Attract 150 unchurched people to the Open Community** [Seeker's Service]
Characteristics of this group:
- unchurched people
- curious about church as a result of a relationship with a member of the core community, or as a result of technigrowth

(4) **Attract 70 people to the New Community**
[Worship Service]
Characteristics of this group:
- must learn and participate in the vision
- should desire to worship God and apply his Word

- should commit to some type of financial support
- should be considering attending community groups

(5) **Form three Community Groups of 12–13 believers** [Small Groups]
Characteristics of this group:
- must attend the open community and new community
- must be willing to participate in and share the vision
- must be willing to help members grow in their relationship with God, with other believers in the group, and with their unchurched friends

Calendar of Events:

August	January	February	March	April	May	June
Sun. 5 Begin Developing CC						
	Sun. 6 20 adults for CC	Sun. 3 CC	Sun. 3 CC	Thur. 4 LC	Wed. 1 First NC CC assimilated into NC	Sun. 2 OC
	Thur. 10 Begin training LC	Thur. 7 LC	Thur. 7 LC	Sun. 7 OC	Thur. 2 LC	Wed. 5 NC
				Wed. 10 CC	Sun. 5 OC	Thur. 6 First CG
	Sun. 13 CC	Sun. 10 CC	Sun. 10 CC	Sun. 14 OC	Wed. 8 NC	Sun. 9 OC
	Mon. 14 Begin Technigrowth LC			Thur. 18 LC	Sun. 12 OC	Wed. 12 NC
					Wed. 15 NC	Sun. 16 OC
					Thur. 16 LC	Wed. 19 NC
						Thur. 20 CG

Sun. 20 CC	Sun. 17 CC	Sun. 17 CC	Sun. 21 OC	Sun. 19 OC	Sun. 23 OC
Thur. 24 LC	Thur. 21 LC	Thur. 21 LC	Wed. 24 CC	Wed. 22 NC	Wed. 26 NC
Sun. 27 CC	Sun. 24 CC	Sun. 24 CC	Sun. 28	Sun. 26 OC	Sun. 30 OC
				Wed. 29 NC	
				Thur. 30 LC	
		Sun. 31 First OC			

Budget:

Personal Expenses: $2,500 per month.
- 40% secular employment
- 20% Core Community support
- 40% Other support (local churches, individuals, etc.)

After first year:
- 70% Midlothian Community Church support
- 30% Other support

Churches Expenses: $16,000 for start up 1/91–6/91
- Technigrowth $5,000
- Publications (bulletins, newsletters, etc.)
                                                                      1,000
- Computer and Printer   4,000
- Audio Visual/Microphones/Music   1,500
- Meeting Facilities   3,500
- Children and Youth*   1,000

                                               $16,000

* A church must care for baby busters, if it is going to reach baby boomers.

Notes

1. Dr. Gary L. McIntosh, The McIntosh Church Growth Network (3630 Camellia Drive, San Bernadino, CA 92404) Volume One Number Two.

2. Dr. Gary L. McIntosh, The McIntosh Church Growth Network (3630 Camellia Drive, San Bernadino, CA 92404) Volume One Number Three.

3. Dallas Seminary Alumni Directory, 1990.

4. Mr. Bill Handley, Driector of Planning and Zoning for Chesterfield County, VA

5. Mr. Bill Handley, Driector of Planning and Zoning for Chesterfield County, VA

6. Mr. Bill Handley, Driector of Planning and Zoning for Chesterfield County, VA

7. Community survey by Christian Fellowship Church, Midlothian, VA

8. Brandermill Community Visitor's Information Packet.

9. Brandermill Community Visitor's Information Packet.

10. Brandermill Community Visitor's Information Packet.

Bitter-Sweet

The Preservation of the Vision

For Pastor Bob, Brother Bill's exodus from the church was bitter-sweet. On the one hand, no one likes to lose, and in a sense Bob felt that he had lost this one. He had hoped that eventually Brother Bill would catch the vision, suit up, and join the team on the field. He realized that this kind of thinking is naive, especially when a visionary takes an established church instead of planting a brand new one. The word is that you "win some, you lose some" in these situations. Pastor Bob, however, was of the temperament that does not like to lose. While he had mellowed somewhat in the last year, his philosophy had always been "Whether it's checkers or church, you play to win or you don't play at all."

He also felt remorse for Bill. He was not quite sure where it came from, for he had not gotten to know him very well. Lord knows, he tried on several occasions, but it seemed as though Bill had erected some kind of barrier between them. He would schedule a breakfast or luncheon with Brother Bill to talk about it, but always, at the last minute, Bill's secretary would call and cancel. One time Bob and Mary had invited him and his wife over for a cookout, but Bill's wife called that morning, apologized, and said they would not be able to make it. She seemed embarrassed and gave no reason for the cancellation. Finally, Bob got the message. Perhaps he would have to be satisfied with the fact that he was not going to be able to reach everyone.

On the other hand, Brother Bill's exodus was sweet. Both Pastor Bob and the board would not have to sit and listen to all of Bill's objections as to why they should not move into the twenty-first century. All had grown extremely weary of it. There was concern that Brother Bill would take some people with him. Indeed, a small group of people in the church felt the same way Brother Bill did. At least he said they did. And the men on the board sensed that this was true, because several had voiced some objections to the "new direction" of the church. But they knew that there were not as many people as Bill implied. Several of the men smiled when Bill or the people used the term "new direction." They thought to themselves, "A new direction implies there was an old direction. We never had any direction to begin with."

But why did Brother Bill leave the church? What events had led up to his departure? Brother Bill continued to protest and voice his opposition to the vision of the church in spite of the fact that most on the board had joined the team as it moved down the field toward the goal. One or two appeared on occasion to drag their heels, but they were in general agreement with the rest of the board as a whole. Pastor Bob knew he could live with that, but he was not sure he could live in the same church with Bill. He did not mind someone playing the game of "devil's advocate," because at times that had caused them to rethink what would have turned out to be a bad decision.

But Brother Bill had a different agenda. He could not "for the life of him" handle change in the church. He could at work, but that was not "God's business." Pastor Bob felt that Bill was not able to distinguish between eternal biblical truth and the culture of the church. For example, when he argued that the organ and the piano were the only acceptable musical instruments for the worship of the church, one of his favorite expressions was, "If it was good enough for Jesus and Paul, it ought to be good enough for us." Most of the men laughed, but not Brother Bill; he believed it.

Pastor Bob knew he could live with this. What angered him and others was that Bill had begun to recruit a following of like-minded people within the church. When he realized that he was alone on the board in his opposition, he began to look for others who felt the same way or had some "beef" with the board. While this was not a large group, his behavior was clearly in violation of the biblical caution to pursue unity (Eph. 4:1–3; Col. 3:14, 15). This both angered and discouraged Pastor Bob.

At first, he was not sure what he should do, so he prayed a lot and read his Bible. It seemed as though God guided him to certain, significant passages of Scripture, in particular the Book of Nehemiah. He also called and met with some older pastor friends and a seminary prof or two for whom he had much respect. From these sources he gained the wisdom and insight for what he had to do. And what was that? What had he learned?

The Problem

Pastor Bob discovered another aspect to the implementation of a vision that few people ever talked about. It is the preservation of the vision. Actually, this is the continuing implementation of the vision. It looks at the envisioning process as a continuing process that takes place throughout the life of the ministry and seeks to facilitate that process in the face of obstacles. The focus in chapters 7 and 8 was on building a ministry team that can deal with obstacles to the accomplishment of the vision. However, the focus of this chapter is on helping visionary leaders, or point people in particular, to deal with specific kinds of obstacles (certain people and events) that are sure to surface in their personal lives and ministries as they lead their teams down the field toward the goal line. These obstacles not only can kill a vision, but they have been known to drive men and women from the ministry. The primary problem is that these obstacles, either separately or together, bring overwhelming discouragement into the visionary's life.

Discouragement

Visionary leaders on the one hand will (not may) face opposition to their ideas and visions. Of course, this news is old news to Bob. His response might be, "Tell me something I don't already know." The problem, on the other hand, concerns their response to that opposition. Most often the initial response is anger followed by discouragement (Neh. 4:5; 6:9). This anger can be good, because it has the potential to bring intensity to the vision. However, the discouragement can be bad, because it can mean the death of the vision. I refer, for example, to the young church planting pastor who, as I mentioned in an earlier chapter, dropped out of the ministry entirely because of his overwhelming discouragement.

Human Sources of Discouragement

Pastor Bob also learned that there are a variety of sources of discouragement. Often discouragement originates with people, either outside or within the ministry organization or both. Most of Nehemiah's opposition came from Israel's unbelieving enemies such as Sanballat, Tobiah, and Geshem (Neh. 2:19; 4:1–8). They used such devices as ridicule (2:19; 4:1–6), conspiracy, (4:7–10), and rumor (4:11, 12).

However, much opposition can surface among those who are a part of the organization. This happened to Nehemiah (Neh. 6:10–13), and it happened, of course, to Pastor Bob. Opposition from without can be beneficial, because it angers and catalyzes people to accomplish the vision. Unreasonable, misguided opposition from people within the ministry often causes the most damage emotionally and spiritually to the visionary leader. I refer to these individuals as vision vampires, vision vultures, and vision firemen.

VISION VAMPIRES. Vision vampires are people who either intentionally or unintentionally attempt to suck the life-blood from the vision. They often are well-intentioned Christians who sincerely believe they are correct in opposing the vision. Often they see themselves as courageous defenders of the faith rather than defenders of the status quo, for many of them confuse the status quo with the faith. In their thinking, somehow liberalism has crept into the organization.

This means that often they will come out of their corner fighting, and fighting hard, because they put visionary leaders in practically the same corner as theological heretics. Both must be fought with gusto if the church is to keep the faith. They seldom verbalize all this, and most would not use the term *heretic* of the leader, for they have no scriptural support, but their behavior betrays their attitudes.

VISION VULTURES. Vision vultures are similar to the vampires but with less intensity. They attack the vision not by sucking the lifeblood from it but by attempting to pick it apart. They are "nitpickers." They do not view visionary leaders as heretics, nor do they see themselves as crusaders who are defending the faith. They do not view change as unbiblical, nor do they call into question the dream on theological grounds. These are people who like things the way they are, because they feel so intimidated and threatened by change.

In the church these people have become accustomed to sitting in pews, passing an offering plate, listening to organ music and long, loud sermons. It is not that the vision is wrong for everybody; they see it as wrong for themselves. Consequently, they attack the vision not as a whole but in parts. They attempt to pick it apart one piece at a time. For a while they may complain about the sermons and how they have changed. Next, they will complain about the instruments and music used in the worship service. And this may go on and on for years.

VISION FIREMEN. Vision firemen are leaders or, better, managers in the organization who, when they hear of a good vision, run and grab the nearest fire hose to put it out. You would hope that because they are in leadership positions they might ignite some fires, but since they are firemen they are much better at putting them out.

They are pure managers in leadership positions who do not properly understand leadership and its relationship to management. As managers, they correctly strive to produce orderly results, not change. Their favorite Bible text is 1 Corinthians 14:40. However, they feel threatened by innovative dreams and believe that it is in their vested interests to protect institutions from change rather than work with leaders to procure change. Since they so often are in high positions in ministry organizations, they can exert a chilling effect on dreaming and those who dare to do so.

RECOGNITION. But how can you discover who the vision opponents are before they have had time to inflict a lot of damage? The key is to listen carefully to the water that flows from the fire hose. These vision opponents often reveal themselves by what they say when they have opportunity to respond to the dream. One popular, time-worn statement is, "We've never done it that way before." This is infamously known among visionary church leaders as the "seven last words of the church." But that is the point. The purpose behind good visionary thinking is to be innovative and come up with new ways of doing things that are more relevant to today's fast-changing culture.

Another common quote is, "We might fail." People in general and some leaders in particular fear failure to such an extent that they will not take risks. Some leaders believe that when they fail they damage their credibility as leaders. While it is true that failure can damage leadership credibility, not to take good risks is to fail.[1] Most great leaders talk about how important failure is to their success. In many cases, they not only learn from their failure but that failure motivates success. The key is to create an environment in which it is permissible to fail.

Another popular nonvisionary quote is, "It's impossible." But this is true of all big visions. In a very real sense that is how you know God is in it. He is in the business of making the impossible possible. Because I have worked with the *Myers-Briggs Temperament Inventory,* I realize that this response is fairly typical of those who prefer to perceive the world primarily through using the five senses, whereas those who prefer to perceive through intuition naturally tend to be more visionary.

Some other quotes you may hear are: "Some people won't like it." "We can't afford it." "You're a dreamer." Brother Bill used some of these and invented a few new ones as well. When you hear these used, especially if they are used repeatedly, the chances are good that you are listening to a vision adversary. Interestingly, all of these quotes are true statements. Visions always invite opposition and are not affordable, and visionaries are dreamers. The problem is that these quotes are seldom placed in their proper context. If we never did things because some people would not like them, then nothing would ever be accomplished. There is always somebody who does not like what you are doing. Many of the things we accomplish in life on the surface appear not affordable. And most good leaders, especially the entrepreneurial type, spend a lot of time dreaming. This was true of Albert Einstein, who on one occasion said that in his work imagination was more important than information.

In his excellent book on paradigms and the change process entitled *Discovering the Future* Joel Arthur Barker lists the following quotes used by those in the prevailing paradigm community (which is often loaded with vision adversaries) against paradigm shifters (visionaries):

"Why, that's impossible."
"We don't do things that way."
"It's too radical a change."

"We tried something like that before, and it didn't work."

"We would be the laughingstock."

"I wish it were that easy."

"It's against accepted policy."

"I always thought you were a little weird."

"Who told you you could change the rules?"

"Let's get back to reality."

"How dare you suggest that what we're doing is wrong?"

and the archetypical response:

"If you had been in this field as long as I have, you would know that what you are suggesting is absolutely absurd."[2]

Other Sources of Discouragement

Sources of discouragement other than people can be failure, fear, fatigue, and frustration. They may often involve people. For example, people may frustrate us or cause us fear. However, they are part of the situations that often bring discouragement into our lives. Whenever visionary leaders become discouraged it will most likely involve one of these four or a combination thereof.

FAILURE. This is illustrated in Nehemiah 4:7–10 where Israel's enemies Sanballat, Tobiah, and others conspired to attack the Jews in Jerusalem. The news of this conspiracy took a heavy toll of discouragement on the people. One result was the potential failure of the vision, for they said, "And we ourselves are unable to rebuild the wall." It is true that we can learn from failure, and good leaders are motivated by failure. But failure can sap people's confidence as well and discourage them from attempting to realize the vision as it did the Jews in Nehemiah's day.

FEAR. While failure teaches and motivates, fear discourages and even paralyzes. It has the awesome potential to make cowards of us all. To distract them from their vision, Sanballat, Tobiah, and the rest conspired to attack and kill the Jews (Neh. 4:7–11). When word arrived in Jerusalem, Nehemiah was forced to act quickly to counter the fear that was building in his people.

Later Sanballat tried a different ploy, threatening to send a false message to Artaxerxes that Nehemiah was planning to set himself up as a king in Jerusalem. Artaxerxes would react quickly and brutally. Nehemiah responded quickly. He explained (Neh. 6:9), "For all of them were trying to frighten us, thinking, 'They will become discouraged with the work and it will not be done.'"

FATIGUE. Fatigue also discouraged the Jews under Nehemiah's leadership. According to Nehemiah 4:10 the people were beginning to lose physical strength, which contributed to their general discouragement. Our bodies must rest at times if we are to serve our Savior with excellence. When fatigue sets in, we become more vulnerable to our sinful natures and discouragement in general. I suspect this is what the Savior had in mind in Matthew 26:40–45 and particularly in verse 41 where he says, "Keep watching and praying, that you may not enter into temptation; the spirit is willing, but the flesh is weak." In times of discouragement, perhaps the best thing to do is go to bed and get some needed rest.

FRUSTRATION. The frustration recorded in Nehemiah 4:10, 11 resulted from a combination of several factors. Although the Jews were physically fatigued and the work was coming to a stop, much work had to be done to clear away all the rubble. Add to this a frustrating environment of fear in that their enemies had threatened their lives, and the result could be the death of the vision, for they had stopped rebuilding the wall (v. 15).

The Solution

I stated at the beginning of this chapter that an often overlooked aspect of the envisioning process is the preservation of the vision. A ministry organization can be well on its way to the realization of its vision, when certain obstacles surface and overwhelm the visionary leader, which results in the untimely death of the vision. The primary obstacle is discouragement.

I believe that more leaders drop out of the ministry because of discouragement than any other problem in ministry, including immorality or the mishandling of the organization's funds. Indeed, discouragement will be one of the great tests of a visionary leader and his or her leadership. What should leaders do when they find themselves deeply discouraged and ready to quit?

The obvious solution to discouragement is encouragement. But what is encouragement all about, and how can leaders find encouragement when they face obstacle-giants in their ministries? Several biblical principles lead to the encouragement of visionary leaders when applied to their situations.

Recognize that Discouragement Is Universal

One truth visionaries must realize is that everyone becomes discouraged. It hits everyone, like death and taxes. Even the apostle Paul, the epitome of visionary leaders (Eph. 3:20), experienced discouragement. Again, it is not a question of *if* but *when*.

This awareness can give a leader hope when discouragement strikes. He realizes that he is no different from anyone else. Moses, David, Paul, Luther, and many others have walked where he walks treading knee deep in the waters of discouragement. Paul obviously spoke from experience when in 1 Corinthians 10:13 he wrote, "No temptation has overtaken you but such as is common to man." Certainly, discouragement would be included under the broad category of temptation.

But not only did they experience it, they survived it. They lived to see another day. If they survived it, there is no reason to think we will not survive it as well. Perhaps the more important issue for leaders who are responsible for implementing dreams is not *if* they will survive it, but *how* they survive it. Will they come through it with their vision still intact, or will it die?

Remember the Lord

Remember the Lord in times of intense discouragement, especially those coming from fear. Nehemiah implemented this practice when he said to his people, "Do not be afraid of them; remember the Lord who is great and awesome, and fight for your brothers, your sons, your daughters, your wives, and your houses" (Neh. 4:14). I believe that what Nehemiah had in mind here is the fact that in times of intense discouragement we forget about God because we become so focused on ourselves and our own difficult circumstances. We have to be reminded of God and the truth of his awesome goodness and greatness and that we have a good God who is on our side in the midst of our discouragement. We need to remember this in light of three contexts.

PAST GOODNESS. God has demonstrated his awesome goodness to us in the past. It is most helpful, especially in times of discouragement, to pause and count all of God's past blessings in our lives. We can begin with the ultimate in blessings, our conversion to Christ and all that is associated with that life-changing event. But that is only the beginning. He continues to pour out his blessings on us in answered prayers, special friends, physical safety, good health, and many other ways.

PRESENT GOODNESS. God continues to demonstrate that goodness in the present, particularly in the blessing of his special abiding presence in our lives. In Hebrews 13:5, 6 the writer says: "Let your character be free from the love of money, being content with what you have; for He Himself has said, 'I will never desert you, nor will I ever forsake you,' so that we confidently say, 'The Lord is my helper, I will not be afraid. What shall man do to me?'"

According to the New Testament, this is a promise for all believers since the cross. However, in the Old Testament it was a special promise to God's visionary leaders such as Moses and Joshua (Josh. 1:5, 9). In the midst of our present discouragement and difficulty, when we may have even forgotten God, he has not forgotten or abandoned us. He will never leave nor forsake us, and we will never experience discouragement and difficulty alone.

FUTURE GOODNESS. God will not cease to pour out his goodness in the future. Because he will not abandon us, even when we leave him, Paul says, we cannot be separated from the love of Christ in our eternal state (Rom. 8:35, 36, 38, 39). Therefore, he concludes, in verse 37, that "in all these things we overwhelmingly conquer through Him who loved us." Regardless of our circumstances, Paul says, we can view ourselves as conquerors in light of our position in Christ. Therefore, no matter what happens or how discouraged we may become, ultimately we win.

Ask God for Strength

Pray and ask God for the strength necessary to overcome the discouragement. In the Old Testament, Nehemiah prayed in the midst of the attempts of his enemies to discourage him and his people from the vision. He told God: "For all of them were trying to frighten us, thinking, 'They will become discouraged with the work and it will not be done.' But now, O God, strengthen my hands" (Neh. 6:9).

But what does that mean? How did God strengthen Nehemiah? David, who was no stranger to discouragement, offered a similar prayer in Psalm 138. In this thanksgiving Psalm, God answered his prayer by strengthening his soul, which resulted in special boldness or courage, for he said, "On the day I called Thou didst answer me; Thou didst make me bold with strength in my soul." Nehemiah's reference to his hands was probably a figure of speech for the work of his hands. He asked God in the midst of his discouraging circumstances to give him boldness or courage as he was about the business of leading his people in the rebuilding of the wall.

The New Testament equivalent to Nehemiah 6:9 is found in 2 Timothy 4:17. Paul was discouraged, because many of his friends had abandoned him (4:10, 16), his enemies were attacking him (4:14, 15), he was in jail, and his death was imminent (4:6, 7). After detailing all this he gave the solution for his discouragement: "But the Lord stood with me, and strengthened me, in order that through me the proclamation might be fully accomplished, and that all the Gentiles might hear; and I was delivered out of the lion's mouth." Paul, like Nehemiah and David, received an infusion of strength necessary from God to accomplish their visions. Here Paul's vision was the proclamation of the gospel to the Gentiles that they might be saved (in essence the Great Commission).

"Hang Tough"

Visionary leaders must not give up on their visions in discouraging situations. They must "hang tough"; they must not be quick to quit. Discouragement hits us emotionally much like a blow to the solar plexus; it knocks the emotional wind out of us. The result is that while we are down for the count, we are greatly tempted to give up on our dreams for God and not get up.

Rather than throw in the towel, God wants us to come up fighting. A great example of this tenacity is Nehemiah's leadership throughout the book. Nehemiah was a fighter, as seen in Nehemiah 4:14 where he not only challenges his people to remember the Lord, but adds, "and fight for your brothers, your sons, your daughters, your wives, and your houses."

The apostle Paul was also a fighter and a finisher. At the end of his life he uses the metaphor of the boxer and runner:

"I have fought the good fight, I have finished the course, I have kept the faith" (2 Tim. 4:7). And perhaps the motivation behind these metaphors is the hope found in 1 Corinthians 10:13 where he says: "No temptation has overtaken you but such as is common to man; and God is faithful, who will not allow you to be tempted beyond what you are able, but with the temptation will provide the way of escape also, that you may be able to endure it." Discouragement most certainly would be included within the broad category of temptation. Therefore, we need to be patient and "hang tough" and not quit, because God says we can endure it.

I stated earlier in this chapter that overwhelming discouragement has eliminated many leaders from ministry. Consequently, I would suggest that the visionary leader not make any major decisions, such as leaving a ministry, while he is discouraged. We must keep in mind that we are not in the right frame of mind when we are discouraged and possibly depressed. Our decisions, whether big or small, will be skewed and based on our circumstances, which are not good. Would we have made the same decision when encouraged? It is best to wait until we have applied some of the principles of this chapter and are in a better frame of mind before we make any major life-affecting decisions.

However, no matter how important or how high a person's leadership position in an organization, he will remain human and fail on occasions. This means that sometimes he may allow discouragement to get the best of him and give up and quit. The problem is that quitting only makes matters worse and adds guilt to that discouragement. But all is not lost. God has made provision for his people's failures at the cross of Christ, and offers his forgiveness. John wrote: "If we confess our sins, He is faithful and righteous to forgive us our sins and to cleanse us from all unrighteousness" (1 John 1:9). David wrote in Psalm 32:5: "I acknowledged my sin to Thee, and my iniquity I did not hide; I said, 'I will confess my transgressions to the Lord'; and Thou didst forgive the guilt of my sin." We all must confess our failures to our forgiving, loving God and experience his forgiveness. Then we take back our towel, climb back in the ring, and continue the fight.

While God is quick to forgive, people may not be. Therefore, it is not always possible or wise to continue in the same ministry. Things that are said and done in the midst of discouragement often run deep emotionally and affect others in leaders' families. They may never heal while in the same ministry, or take so long to heal that it is best to move to a new ministry organization with a new team of people. Also, visionary leaders may have to settle for a position other than primary leader for a period of time until they prove themselves again.

Encourage Others

Visionary leaders should make a point of encouraging others. Paul issues a general exhortation to those in the church at Thessalonica to encourage one another (1 Thess. 5:11). In Hebrews 3:13, the writer does the same to those who were tempted to fall away from the living God. However, on several occasions Paul specifically sent certain leaders to encourage the saints. For example, he sent Timothy to Thessalonica so that he might strengthen and encourage them in their faith (1 Thess. 3:2). Again, he sent Tychicus to the believers at Colossae to update them on Paul's circumstances and to encourage their hearts (Col. 4:7, 8).

Visionary leaders only experience discouragement at certain times, not all the time. Therefore, they know and understand what it is like for other leaders to go through difficult, discouraging times in their lives and ministries. Therefore, like Barnabas in Acts 11:22, 23, an important aspect of their own ministries is to look for and seek to encourage other leaders who become discouraged and are ready to quit. In short, be an encourager.

Spend Time with Visionaries

Visionaries prevent discouragement in their lives by regularly exposing themselves to other visionary people and visionary material. Encouragement is infectious. Therefore, visionary leaders should frequent one another's company and stay abreast of what others are doing in their ministries. Proverbs 27:17 says: "Iron sharpens iron, so one man sharpens another." I have several suggestions.

INDIVIDUAL MEETINGS. First, they can seek out other leaders in ministries similar to theirs or possibly one that is different. Pastors may want to meet with pastors, and parachurch leaders with parachurch leaders. This is because their ministries may have so much in common that they find it a "sharpening" experience when they get together. But it can be most beneficial to meet with those who lead in other organizations as well. Pastors can learn much from parachurch leaders, and both can learn from those who are leading in the business world.

GROUP MEETINGS. Another suggestion is for leaders to meet in groups. I meet once a month with a group of visionaries consisting of pastors and parachurch leaders from several different denominations. What we all have in common is a desire to be on the cutting edge of the Great Commission ministry. Our agenda may vary from a review of the latest Christian or secular book on leadership to bringing in an outside specialist on some pertinent topic.

PASTORS' CONFERENCES. Attend pastors' conferences sponsored by churches that are led by strong visionaries. An excellent conference is the one held by Pastor Bill Hybels and his staff at Willow Creek Community Church in South Barrington, Illinois (a suburb of Chicago). This conference takes place three times a year and limits the number of people who can attend each conference. Another good conference is the one held by Pastor Rick Warren at Saddleback Valley Community Church in Mission Viejo, California. This one is held once a year during the summer with no limitation on the number who can attend. Both of these conferences are sensitive to a typical pastor's salary and attempt to hold costs to a minimum.

TAPE MINISTRIES. Take advantage of the tape ministries of various organizations that are on the cutting edge. Both Willow Creek and Saddleback Valley Community Church provide these services for those interested in pastoral ministries. Another excellent organization is the Charles E. Fuller Institute of Evangelism and Church Growth in Pasadena, California (operated separately from Fuller Seminary, also located in Pasadena).

Dr. John Maxwell, a popular speaker on leadership and the pastor of Skyline Wesleyan Church, makes his tapes available through a ministry organization called Injoy in Spring Valley, California. Also, I have produced some tapes primarily in the area of church planting, which may be ordered through the tape ministry of Dallas Theological Seminary in Dallas, Texas. Some of these organizations provide other materials such as videotapes and written materials.

LITERATURE. Read broadly in areas related to leadership and creativity. Every good visionary leader is a reader. An increasing number of good Christian books are being published on creative leadership. The various Christian publishers will usually provide a catalog on request.

But innovative Christian leaders read good books on business as well. Tom Peters has made an excellent contribution to innovative leadership through several provocative, challenging books and videos. Joel Arthur Barker has written a book and produced a video on paradigms and another video on vision. I have found that a publisher of excellent works on business leadership and management is Jossey-Bass Publishers. Write them for a catalog.

Confront Vision Adversaries

Visionary leaders will encounter visionary vampires, vultures, and firemen who come into their ministries and discourage them. Dealing with fellow believers who oppose changes, for whatever reasons, can be challenging and requires tact, understanding, wisdom, and patience. These are some suggested steps.

MEET IN PRIVATE. The leader must arrange to meet with the vision adversary preferably in private. This is the spirit of the Scriptures according to such passages as Matthew 5:23, 24 and 18:15. It has the advantages of determining if, in fact, there are any differences, getting the parties to deal with their differences, and attempting to resolve the differences without unnecessary publicity for the individual or ministry.

IDENTIFY THE PROBLEM. Try to determine the nature of the problem. Most often it is a difference in the parties' philosophies or personalities, or sin, or a combination thereof.

A philosophical difference between two people can be a problem. I would include under philosophy such matters as a different vision, a different philosophy of ministry, a preference for the status quo, a different interpretation of Scripture, and so on. Usually these are differences of opinion that can be held by two reasonably mature Christians without involving sin on either side. It is important that the two people spend some time together trying to "air out" their differences and arrive at a consensus of opinion in a spirit of love and cooperation. If the person who differs with the ministry leader is also a leader, then a decision will have to be made as to whether or not that person should stay with the ministry or pursue that which is closer to his philosophy in another ministry.

A problem can be a difference in personalities. A general rule is that those with similar personalities get along better than those with differing personalities. Again, it is important that the people involved get together to try to understand one another. God has designed us with different temperaments but with the ability to work together as a team to accomplish a particular vision. Each personality provides an important, necessary ingredient.

Usually when a team of relatively mature people, who understand the importance of these differences, get together to accomplish the same dream, they learn to appreciate the gifts and abilities of the others and value their input. However, if they are unable to resolve their differences, it is to be hoped that the problem is not with the primary leader and his maturity. Assuming this is the case and the other person is also a leader in the organization, it is probably best for the ministry that the other person leaves the organization.

Possibly a problem is due to sin. Some people in ministry organizations are well-intentioned trouble makers. They work their way up through the ranks of a ministry organization until they reach a leadership position. They appear to be loyal to the ministry and are very faithful to it. In the church they are people who carry a Bible and are present at all the meetings of the church. They give regularly and show up on church work days (which in some churches is equated with spirituality). However, these people have a different vision with a different agenda.

They manifest themselves through their constant opposition to the visionary leader and his vision. It becomes obvious that he will not be able to lead them. This is because ultimately they, like Diotrephes in 3 John 9, want to be the ones who lead the organization. They do not want the official title that goes with the primary leadership position such as president or pastor. They are perfectly willing to let someone else wear the title as long as they are the ones who "call the shots."

Usually their strategy involves recruiting and lining up others in the organization behind them and their agenda. These other people are often dissidents themselves who do not like the direction of the ministry organization. These individuals will seek to get what they want through innuendo, spreading false or questionable rumors, and encouraging factions in the organization. They hope to divide and conquer, for if they get enough people on their side they will gain the control they desire to accomplish their ends. I wish this was not the case, but I have been in ministry long enough to know better. I call this the dark side of ministry.

What can a visionary leader do in a situation like this? A lot depends on whether this leader is already in power or not. If he is called to a ministry as the point person, it is always wise to try to determine if a potentially opposing person is already in power. A key here is to ask various people in the organization who has been leading the organization while they were looking for a new leader. If this person is still on the scene, the leader who is considering the appointment should spend some time with him, and he will reveal either subtly or blatantly where he stands. It is best not to take a position in an organization like this in the first place. The leader who is not aware of the situation and winds up in a bad situation may have to resign.

However, if he is already in the point position of a ministry and one of these individuals comes along, the point person must deal with him or her as soon as possible before it is too late. To ignore these people can cost a person his ministry. In Romans 16:17, Paul warns, "Now I urge you, brethren, keep your eye on those who cause dissensions and hindrances contrary to the teaching which you learned, and turn away from them." Again, in Titus 3:10, 11, he advises, "Reject a factious man after a first and second warning, knowing that such a man is perverted and is sinning, being self-condemned." If the person involved has become somewhat rooted in the ministry, then most likely it will be necessary to implement the disciplinary procedures according to Matthew 18:15–20.

RESOLVE THE PROBLEM. Finally, leaders should attempt to resolve any problems. Unresolved personal problems, whether in a ministry, a marriage, or any other relationship, have a way of piling up and coming back to "haunt" them later in their ministries. Scripture commands us to resolve our differences (Matt. 5:24; 18:15). If the other party responds favorably, then we have won back a brother or sister. If that person does not respond, then, as in the worse case scenario above, he must be disciplined.

After thinking this through, Pastor Bob decided that Brother Bill differed with him in philosophy and personality. Bill tenaciously held to the status quo. For him, change was out of the question, at least the kind of changes Pastor Bob envisioned. He wanted to continue with what he called the present vision, which was, in fact, no vision, at least not one that anybody, including Bill, could articulate. When asked to do so, he would say something about "preaching the Word." But Pastor Bob was quick to point out to him that "preaching the Word," which is imperative to any ministry, is a means to an end and not an end in itself.

Pastor Bob also sensed that Bill did not feel and probably would never feel a personal affinity toward him. He observed in the board meetings there was something between them that was difficult to pin down. Brother Bill always seemed to be on the other side of any issue that came up. Sometimes he was correct, but at other times his opposition was irrational. However, the real tip-off was Bill's resistance to meeting with Bob privately.

Because Brother Bill had been in the church from the beginning, Pastor Bob felt that he could live with their differences in philosophy and personality, especially since the agendas of the pastor and the board were now essentially the same. So he decided he would ask Bill to resign from the board but stay in the church. What Bob felt he could not tolerate was Bill's recent recruitment of others whose visions and agendas for the church differed from his. Bill was probably doing this out of desperation, but it was sin and it must be dealt with. He did not look forward to the coming confrontation.

The board meeting was over and most of the men had left. Pastor Bob observed that Brother Bill stayed behind this night to get things ready for his class on Sunday morning. Bob nervously walked into Bill's classroom uttering a quick prayer under his breath and closed the door. Bill looked surprised when Bob entered the room, and then showed some visible nervousness when he closed the door.

For a while the discussion was rather heated as Brother Bill vented his anger. He was a man who was used to having his way, and he let Bob know it. After all, who was he to come in and change this church? Everything was just fine until he came along. Bob listened patiently, even though he felt his own anger welling up inside him. It was all he could do to keep from lashing back at the man. But for once, by God's grace, he managed to stay calm. God was answering all his prayers in anticipation of this event. Instead of responding in kind, he repeatedly asked Bill key, penetrating questions throughout the intense conversation.

Finally, after what seemed like hours, Brother Bill ran out of gas. His mood began to change, he grew quiet, and perhaps for the first time he listened to Pastor Bob. As Bob spoke and observed Bill's reactions, he realized again that basically Bill was a good man who loved God but had in desperation made some bad choices as things in the church began to turn in a new, different direction.

While it was intensely difficult for him, Brother Bill had to admit that he was wrong and had sinned when he approached people in the church and spoke against Pastor Bob and those on the board. Finally, though somewhat reluctantly, he agreed to go back to these people and "set things straight." Also, after further discussion he agreed, miracle of miracles, to apologize to the board and then resign.

It was early in the morning; the sun was just beginning to make its presence known by sending out long rays of light as it began to break above the horizon. The two men walked away from the church facility, climbed into their vehicles, and headed home. Pastor Bob was exhausted but happy and greatly relieved as he thought about all that had just taken place.

Brother Bill was a good man, and he kept his promise. Pastor Bob knew, because word got back to him through various individuals in the church. And, of course, Bob was there at the next board meeting when Bill apologized for his actions to the board. A number of the men were shocked—Bill could see it on their faces—but later rejoiced as they discussed in private what had taken place.

After this, there was a growing unity in the church, which many had not felt since it was first planted. Also, the church was growing even faster as it continued to reach a number of nonchurched people in the community. There was talk of going to three services, and the board had hired an architect to draw up plans to build an addition to the facility. Brother Bill still remained in disagreement with the church's vision, so he and his family quietly left to attend another church in the area.

Developing Your Vision

This worksheet is designed to help you develop your vision. Write down any thoughts or ideas you have at this point. Next, work them through the following steps.

Envisioning Prayer

1. Do you have a daily quiet time for prayer and the study of God's Word?
2. Set aside a portion of that time to pray about your vision.
3. Ask God to give you his vision for your people.
4. Be alert to what comes into your mind during these times.
5. Also, be alert to the people and events he brings into your life.
6. Pray specifically for such things as:

   Wisdom and insight concerning the vision
   The people under your ministry
   Your leadership and that of others on your team
   The potential of your vision

Thinking Big

1. Make sure your vision goes far beyond your own talents and abilities. What aspect of your vision can you reasonably accomplish on your own, and what is beyond your abilities to accomplish?
2. Observe your people's response to your vision as you begin to communicate it. Do you sense that they are challenged or discouraged?

3. Double or triple the size of your present vision. Should this be the size of your dream?
4. Does the size of your vision reflect the size of your God? Based on the size of your dream, how big is your God?
5. What exposure do you have to other people who think big? Name them.

Written Brainstorming

1. Keep some kind of writing material available so that you can write down ideas as God places them on your heart. (Consider a vision notebook, a pad, or a 3" x 5" card file.)
2. Write down anything related to the vision that comes to mind, even if it seems foolish. Reserve judgment until later.
3. Collect other visions, vision slogans, and any information that might be helpful to your vision.

Organizing the Material

1. What is the purpose of your vision? How does it relate to the Great Commission?
2. What are the values of your ministry? List them. Are any unique?
3. What is your strategy? Can you write it out?
4. Who is on your team? Who makes up the target group?
5. What is the site of your ministry?
6. How will this ministry be financed?
7. Which of the above should be included in the vision statement?

Questioning the Dream

1. Is the dream clear? Have you asked anyone else to articulate it back to you?

2. Is it challenging? Do people appear excited when they hear your dream?
3. Is it visual? What do you and others "see" when the vision is communicated?
4. Is it future oriented?
5. Is it realistic yet stretching?
6. Is it culturally relevant?

Demonstrating Patience

1. Do you consider yourself to be a patient person?
2. Are you under any time constraints for the vision? If so, is this reasonable?
3. Are you willing to give the vision whatever time is necessary for its development?

Developing Vision Slogans

Vision slogans usually follow certain patterns. Note the sample patterns; then fill in the spaces under each with your own ideas, concepts, numbers, and so on. Once you feel that you understand the process, create some patterns of your own and develop a vision slogan that is unique to your ministry.

1. Pattern #1: Connect two concepts with the preposition *by*. The first concept may denote a certain number of people and the second a certain year.

   "200 by 2000"

   "_____ by _____"

2. Pattern #2: A variation of pattern #1 precedes the first number with a participle.

   "Reaching 200 for 2000"

   "Reaching _____ for _____"

3. Pattern #3: Begin the slogan with a participle and connect it to an infinitive of purpose. This can be taken to one, two, or as many as three levels.

   "Building a community to reach a community"

   (one level)

   "_____ -ing _____ to _____"

4. Pattern #4: Use the same number, or different numbers, followed by a progression answering the questions about what, where, and when.

   "One _____, one _____, one _____"

5. On a separate sheet of paper establish some patterns of your own. Create your own vision slogan.

Casting Your Vision

This worksheet is designed to help you work through the various steps in the communication of your vision.

1. In every ministry the primary leader is responsible for the communication of the vision. Are you that person? If not, who is? Candidly, is the job being done? Are others in the ministry casting the vision? Why or why not?
2. Are you aware of any critical deficiencies or problems with the status quo that relate in some way to your ministry? What are they? Can you use any of these situations as a context for your vision?
3. Are there any untapped or unexploited opportunities in your community that your ministry could use as a context for casting your dream? Ask some of the people who are a part of your ministry if they are aware of any opportunities. You may find them in your local newspaper.
4. Have you ever sensed God's hand of blessing on you and your ministry in a special way such as Nehemiah experienced? List some of these occurrences.
5. How would you rate yourself as a speaker? Do not be too humble. How does someone else in your ministry who has been exposed to other good speakers rate you? How about your spouse? Are you afraid to ask?
6. What do you do on a regular basis to develop your character and walk with God? If you are "stuck in a rut," read chapter 2 of Bill Hybels' book *Honest to God*. It was developed to help Christians cultivate integrity and a passion for the Savior. Another helpful work is Dallas Willard's *The Spirit of the Disciplines*.

7. Who makes up your ministry community? Who makes up your ministry constituency? Can you visualize either as a vision community or vision constituency?

8. Does your dream excite you? Do you talk about it often with other people who might be interested? Have you ever lain awake at night thinking about it?

9. Have you collected any good vision stories to tell? Are there any ministries similar to yours that excite you and have been obviously blessed of God? What stories can you glean from them?

10. Take a blank sheet of paper and place two headings at the top, one *evangelism* and the other *edification.* List all of your current programs under the appropriate heading. Are the two lists balanced? What unspoken vision do your programs communicate to your people? Is this unspoken vision the same as your spoken vision?

11. Which of the ten practical methods listed in chapter 5 for communicating the vision would work in your situation? What other practical methods popped into your mind as you read through the ten? Did you write them down in the margin of the book? If you did not, go back and do it now before you forget them.

12. Browse through several magazines, clip-art books, and advertisements. Do you spot any logos that give you some ideas for one of your own?

13. How well do you understand the felt needs and aspirations of those under your ministry? Make a list of them. Was this difficult or easy? Carefully quiz some of the people under your ministry with the same question. Do their answers match yours?

Building a Team 1

Evaluating Your Group

1. On a blank sheet of paper draw two horizontal lines from one side of the page to the other about one or two inches apart. Place the numerals 1 through 10 from left to right on both lines. Write *commitment* above the first line and *cooperation* above the second.
2. Choose the appropriate number on the scale that rates as a whole the group you are working with in terms of their commitment to each other and the vision, and their cooperation in the same (1 is the lowest, 10 is highest).
3. In the same way rate each individual in the group including yourself.
4. If your group scored under 5 as a whole, you need to answer several key questions.
   a) How long have you been with this ministry?
   b) Do you understand how to build a group into a team?
   c) Have you been with this group long enough that you should have seen some progress by now?
   d) Do these people need more time? If your answer is yes, are you being realistic?
   e) Do you see progress or growth on the part of the group as a whole or in the lives of certain individuals?
   f) Is it time to consider another ministry?
5. Did any of the individuals in the group score below 5?
   a) Why does this person struggle with commitment and cooperation?
   b) Do you believe this person will grow and improve in these areas? Why or why not?

c) How many individuals scored under 5?
d) What are the chances of their leaving the group?
e) Should you consider another ministry?

Building a Team

1. Casting and recasting the dream.
   a) Do you feel that you have a good understanding of your group's needs, hopes, and aspirations for the future? Can you list them?
   b) Have you cast your vision in such a way that your group sees how it relates to their needs, hopes, and aspirations?
2. Creating a climate of trust and vulnerability.
   a) Do you trust the people in your group? Why, or why not?
   b) Do you delegate responsibility to the people in the group? Why, or why not?
   c) Are you vulnerable with your group? Have you ever shared your fears and anxieties with them as a group or individually? Why, or why not?
   d) Do you encourage others in the group to participate in the decision-making process, especially in the areas of their expertise?
3. Developing a sense of community or team spirit.
   a) Monitor your speech when you are around your group for one week. If this is too difficult for you, ask someone else such as your spouse or secretary to do it for you.
   b) When you are with your group, what kinds of pronouns do you use? Are they *I* and *my* or *we* and *our?*
   c) How much time do you spend together with your group? Is it mostly for business or pleasure or both? Do you ever have fun together away from the office?

d) How much time do you spend with the individuals who make up the group? Does it include pleasure as well as business? Have you ever invited any into your home for some fellowship and fun? Do you find yourself avoiding anyone in particular? Who is it? Why? Are your reasons valid?

4. Keeping the lines of communication open.

   a) How well does your team communicate?

   b) Are you aware of any unresolved conflicts between people in your group including yourself?

   c) When there is a conflict, do the people in your group go to one another privately to seek resolution?

Building a Team 2

This worksheet is for the visionary leader who has developed a vision and is in the process of building a team to accomplish a vision. It seeks to help you handle "obstinate obstacles" that will affect the implementation of the vision.

Empowering the Team

1. Make a list of the obstacles that you and your team face as you attempt to implement your ministry team. You may want to do this by yourself and then together with your team to get their perspective. Which will prove difficult for your team to overcome?
2. As soon as possible teach your team the critical principles of the grace of God in Jesus Christ. In analyzing yourself and those on the team, do you sense that any are struggling with their self-esteem regarding their performance, acceptance, blame, or shame, or a combination thereof?
3. Do you have a program to help your team and any others in your ministry to discover their divine design and their ministry niche?
4. At present, would you consider yourself a servant-leader? Why or why not? Would the others on your team? Would you be willing to ask their opinion? Are you in a position in your ministry where you can pour a substantial amount of your time into the lives of your ministry team? Why or why not? What would you have to do to make this possible? Are you willing to do whatever it takes to make this a reality?
5. Review the responsibilities of those on the ministry team including your own. Are there any areas or

responsibilities you can break down into "bite-size" tasks?

6. Where is the power in your ministry organization, and who has the authority to exercise that power? Is it possible to delegate power and the authority to exercise that power to those who lead in a particular ministry area?

7. Do you now model the values you affirm in your ministry? Would you be willing to say to your team, "Be imitators of me, just as I also am of Christ"?

Encouraging the Team

1. How do you deal with personal and team discouragement in your ministry organization? What possible discouragement do you and your team now face?

2. Do you have in place both a formal and an informal award system? Are you the team cheerleader? Do you and your team ever celebrate your accomplishments? Name some of the ways in which you do this.

Planning Your Ministry

1. Collect as many planning documents as possible from both church and parachurch organizations. You now have at least one document for your collection, the one from Midlothian Community Church. Ultimately, the majority should be for your particular ministry. If you are in a multi-staff ministry, it might be wise to have the others do this for their ministry areas.
2. Sort through these and determine and mark which you like best and why.
3. Carve out one day from your busy schedule for planning and write it on your calendar. It might be helpful to get away for that day.
4. Construct a basic outline for your plan (need, vision, strategy, goals, calendar of events, and budget). Place the information from the other documents and any other relevant information on the outline. It might be helpful to cut some of this information and paste it on a large sheet containing the outline.
5. After you have had sufficient time to think through the results, type this information in the format that appeals most to you. Periodically review and update it.
6. At the next board or ministry team retreat, present this plan to your people as a worksheet. Ask them to add, delete, or change anything in the document. Discuss any changes with them.
7. Type up the final plan and take it to a professional for the additional art work and graphics to make the plan visually attractive.
8. Submit copies to all who are involved in implementing the plan. Be ready to monitor, explain, troubleshoot, and change the plan periodically.

Preserving Your Vision

1. Are you often discouraged in your ministry? Where would you place discouragement in your list of major ministry problems? Is it your main problem?
2. What are the sources of your discouragement? Do you face any vision vampires, vultures, or firemen? If so, what are these persons' names? Have you any other sources of discouragement such as failure, fear, fatigue, or frustration? Which one(s)? Can you pin your discouragement down to any one particular obstacle or combination of obstacles? You might find it helpful to express this and your feelings by writing them on paper or in your journal.
3. Check the behaviors you believe might turn your discouragement into encouragement. Be sure to put them into practice now and whenever you feel discouraged.

Recognize that discouragement is universal.

Remember the Lord.

Ask for strength.

"Hang tough."

Encourage others.

Spend time with visionaries and their materials.

Confront vision adversaries.

Endnotes

Chapter 1 *It's a Must!*

1. George Barna, *The Frog in the Kettle* (Ventura, Calif.: Regal Books, 1990), p. 142.
2. Ibid., p. 49.
3. In an attempt to be both relevant and sensitive to their culture, some ministries describe themselves as market driven. I believe this is a mistake. They should be what I refer to as "vision driven, market sensitive."

Chapter 2 *What Are We Talking About?*

1. I would like to give credit to my friend and former student, Mike Baer, for his thinking in this area, which has influenced me.
2. John R. W. Stott, "What Makes Leadership Christian?" *Christianity Today*, August 1985, p. 24.

Chapter 3 *Giving Birth: Part 1*

1. Peter Wagner provides an excellent discussion of this concept and its historical development in America in his book *Leading Your Church to Growth* (Ventura, Calif.: Regal Books, 1984), pp. 73–105.
2. Isabel Briggs Myers, *Gifts Differing* (Palo Alto, Calif.: Consulting Psychologists Press, 1980), p. 2.
3. Isabel Briggs Myers and Mary H. McCaulley, *Manual: A Guide to the Development and Use of the Myers-Briggs Type Indicator* (Palo Alto, Calif.: Consulting Psychologists Press, 1985), pp. 45, 47.
4. The MBTI can be administered at most psychological counseling centers and some assessment centers. It should be administered only by someone who has met all the qualifications of the Association for Psychological Type (APT).
5. Myers and McCaulley, *Manual*, p. 14.
6. Jay Conger, The *Charismatic Leader* (San Francisco, Calif.: Jossey-Bass Publishers, 1989), p. 65.
7. James M. Kouzes and Barry Z. Posner, *The Leadership Challenge* (San Francisco, Calif.: Jossey-Bass Publishers, 1987), p. 94.
8. Fred Smith, *Learning to Lead* (Waco.: Word Books, 1986), p. 38.
9. Ibid.

Chapter 4   *Giving Birth: Part 2*

1. In my work with students at Dallas Theological Seminary, I have discovered exceptions among those who score as S's and C's on the *Personal Profile* but show a preference for intuition on the *Myers-Briggs Temperament Inventory* (MBTI).

2. John Haggai, *Lead On!* (Waco : Word Books, 1986), p. 14.

3. Warren Bennis and Burt Nanus, *Leaders* (New York, N.Y.: Harper & Row, 1985), p. 95.

4. Ibid., p. 96.

5. Dallas Theological Seminary 1990–91 Catalog, p. 6.

6. Bill Bright, *Come Help Change the World* (San Bernardino, Calif.: Here's Life Publishers, Inc., 1979), p. 7.

7. George Gallup, Jr., *The Unchurched American—Ten Years Later* (Princeton, N.J.: The Princeton Religion Research Center, 1988), p. 2.

8. George Barna, *The Frog in the Kettle* (Ventura, Calif.: Regal Books, 1990), p. 142.

9. Gallup, Ibid., p. 4.

10. Pastor Stevens's material in this chapter is used by permission.

11. John Madden, with Dave Anderson, *Hey, Wait a Minute* (New York: Ballantine, 1985), pp. 225–226.

Chapter 5   *It's a Vision!*

1. George Gallup, Jr., The *Unchurched American—Ten Years Later* (Princeton, NJ.: The Princeton Religion Research Center, 1988), p. 3.

2. George Barna, *Successful Churches: What They Have in Common* (Glendale, Calif.: The Barna Research Group), p. 15.

3. Jay A. Conger, *The Charismatic Leader* (San Francisco: Jossey–Bass Publishers, 1989), p. 78.

4. James M. Kouzes and Barry Z. Posner, *The Leadership Challenge* (San Francisco: Jossey-Bass Publishers, 1987), pp. 123–24.

5. Ibid., p. 124.

6. Advertising agencies and free-lance artists do not have to be expensive, either. When you consider the value of a good logo to the organization, the result is well worth the expense.

Chapter 6   *Overcoming Initial Inertia*

1. John P. Kotter, *A Force for Change* (New York: The Free Press, 1990), p. 7.

2. Ibid., p. 5.

3. Ibid., p. 4.

4. Ibid., p. 63.

5. Ibid., p. 5.

6. James M. Kouzes and Barry Z. Posner, *The Leadership Challenge* (San Francisco: Jossey-Bass Publishers, 1987), pp. 137–38.

7. Ibid., p. 153.

8. John Naisbitt and Patricia Aburdene, *Megatrends 2000* (New York: William Morrow and Company, Inc., 1990), p. 227.

9. Ibid.

Chapter 7 *Overcoming Obstinate Obstacles*

1. Jay A. Conger, *The Charismatic Leader* (San Francisco: Jossey-Bass Publishers, 1989), p. 108.

2. Ibid.

3. Ibid., p. 109.

4. Robert S. McGee, *The Search for Significance* (Houston: Rapha Publishing, 1990), p. 15.

5. Ibid., ch. 6.

6. Ibid., ch. 7.

7. Ibid., ch. 8.

8. Ibid., ch. 9.

9. This is one of the statements my friend, Pastor Bruce Bugby of Willow Creek Community Church, has chosen to communicate this concept.

10. Robert E. Coleman, *The Master Plan of Evangelism* (Old Tappan, N.J.: Fleming H. Revell Company, 1963), p. 43.

11. Ibid., pp. 40–41.

12. James M. Kouzes and Barry Z. Posner, *The Leadership Challenge* (San Francisco: Jossey-Bass, 1987), p. 218.

13. Ibid., p. 221.

14. Ibid., p. 195.

15. Ibid., p. 260.

16. Ibid., p. 242.

17. Ibid., p. 260, 263.

Chapter 8 *Wearing the Management Hat*

1. John P. Kotter, *A Force for Change* (New York: The Free Press, 1990), pp. 3–4. Also, pp. 12–18 provide more historical background.

2. Leith Anderson, *Dying for Change* (Minneapolis: Bethany House Publishers, 1990), pp. 9–10.

3. Ibid., p. 10.

4. Kotter, *A Force for Change*, p. 7.

5. George Barna, *The Frog in the Kettle* (Ventura, Calif.: Regal Books, 1990), p. 223.

6. Ibid.

7. Tom Peters has addressed this issue in his book *Thriving on Chaos* (New York: Harper & Row, 1987).

8. Peter Wagner has a good section on these gifts and their relationship to leadership in *Leading Your Church to Growth* (Ventura, Calif.: Regal Books, 1984), pp. 87–89.

9. Kotter, *A Force for Change*, p. 39.

10. Ibid., p. 39.

11. I use it here with his permission.

Midlothian Community Church Insert

1. Dr. Gary L. McIntosh, *The McIntosh Church Growth Network* (3630 Camellia Drive, San Bernardino, CA 92404) Volume One Number Two.
2. Dr. Gary L. McIntosh, *The McIntosh Church Growth Network* (3630 Camellia Drive, San Bernardino, CA 92404) Volume One Number Three.
3. Dallas Seminary Alumni Directory, 1990.
4. Mr. Bill Handley, Director of Planning and Zoning for Chesterfield County, VA.
5. Mr. Bill Handley, Director of Planning and Zoning for Chesterfield County, VA.
6. Mr. Bill Handley, Director of Planning and Zoning for Chesterfield County, VA.
7. Community survey by Christian Fellowship Church, Midlothian, VA.
8. Brandermill Community Visitor's Information Packet.
9. Brandermill Community Visitor's Information Packet.
10. Brandermill Community Visitor's Information Packet.

Chapter 9   *Bitter-sweet*

1. Good risks are hard to determine and vary from person to person. What may be a good risk for one leader may not be for another. Tom Peters has a brief but helpful discussion of what I call good risk-taking in *Thriving on Chaos* (New York: Harper & Row, 1987), pp. 322–23.
2. Joel Arthur Barker, *Discovering the Future: The Business of Paradigms* (St. Paul, Minn.: ILI Press, 1985), pp. 30–31.